LOOSE PARTS *Alive*

Inspiring *Child-Led* *Nature* Explorations

by Carla Gull, EdD *and* Laura Wilhelm, EdD

Copyright

Published by Gryphon House, Inc.
P. O. Box 10, Lewisville, NC 27023
800.638.0928; 877.638.7576 [fax]
Visit us on the web at www.gryphonhouse.com.

Library of Congress Control Number: 2024932348

Bulk Purchase

Gryphon House books are available for special premiums and sales promotions as well as for fund-raising use. Special editions or book excerpts also can be created to specifications. For details, call 800.638.0928.

Disclaimer

Gryphon House, Inc., cannot be held responsible for damage, mishap, or injury incurred during the use of or because of activities in this book. Appropriate and reasonable caution and adult supervision of children involved in activities and corresponding to the age and capability of each child involved are recommended at all times. Do not leave children unattended at any time. Observe safety and caution at all times.

LOOSE PARTS *Alive*

Inspiring *Child-Led Nature* Explorations

by Carla Gull, EdD *and* Laura Wilhelm, EdD

TABLE *of* CONTENTS

Preface

When catastrophe strikes, some people are able to draw on inner reserves of strength and prior experiences to assess the situation and make a plan for their own survival while assisting others. Teachers and other helping professionals are especially skilled at these tasks. We've listened to the flight attendants' instructions. We know to put on our own oxygen mask first and breathe normally. Yet with the global pandemic, very few of us had any similar experiences to fall back on. The rules had not been printed on the seatback card and were changing on us mid-flight. As adults, we found ourselves sandwiched between needing to care for and protect young children, as well as elderly friends and relatives, while learning to navigate almost universal uncertainty and changes affecting everything from our jobs to how to find groceries. In the United States, many parents also became responsible for keeping older children focused on virtual schooling and caring for babies and toddlers while trying to work from home. Although some European countries provided concrete supports for families with young children, pandemic trauma has affected virtually everyone on Earth. Each of us has experienced it differently, but almost no one, from babies to elders, remained unscathed.

As we emerge and recover, we need to recognize the trauma we've all experienced. We need to help children, especially, to process pandemic losses: the lives lost, missed time with relatives, lost schooling, and missed familiar routines. Allowing for therapeutic play honors these losses. We can recognize the trauma we've all been through and give ourselves and the children we care for a little grace. Rather than rushing to fill children with bits of missed information, we need to nurture them and practice slow pedagogy as everyone recovers (Egan et al., 2021). The pandemic can be viewed as a threshold or liminal space that allows us to reconnect with the natural world (Adams and Gray, 2023). Because today's children have missed out on many normal childhood social and language experiences, we must help them build soft skills and firsthand knowledge as a strong foundation for the rest of their learning journey. This is where loose parts fit beautifully. Open-ended play can provide an avenue for young children to try new ideas and practice authentic conversations, because their work gives meaningful context for learning.

Observations from a variety of settings illustrate ways to extend loose parts play beyond a collection of objects into interactive play with living things viewed through a constructivist lens. *Constructivism* refers to psychologist Jean Piaget's concept of a child's skill at creating coherent meaning from scattered facts and applying that information in spontaneous play, problem solving, and self-regulation (Forman and Kuschner, 1983).

Living loose parts play is a catalyst for the spontaneous joy and lively conversations that can begin to address the language loss and social disconnection that has occurred throughout the years of the global pandemic and will continue to affect us all for years to come (Charney, Camarata, and Chern, 2020; Skar, Graham, and Huebner, 2022). Pandemic uncertainty has increased the need for social connections and emotional respite for adults and children. We all need playful learning to sustain our hearts and express ideas through work with our hands.

Acknowledgments

We collaborated on this project with a variety of people who are actively involved with living loose parts. As authors and practitioners, we want to elevate additional voices with rich ideas and diverse perspectives. We are grateful for inspirational conversations with Gary Bilezikian, president of Guidecraft, a producer of educational toys and children's furniture; Chris Whitmire, early childhood district administrator at Lewis Cass ISD in Indiana; Jennifer Kesselring, head of the preschool division of Riverfield Country Day School; Andrine Shufran, coordinator at Oklahoma State University Insect Adventure; Joe Rackley, environmental educator and pest survey coordinator for the state of Oklahoma; and Charlotte Wood-Wilson, retired Montessori professor from Oklahoma City University, whose ideas uplift, inspire, and challenge us at every encounter.

We have sprinkled true stories from the field throughout the text, sharing the author and program as available. We want to honor many voices and points of view as early childhood environmental educators continue to inspire each other.

* **April Zajko, MEd, Nature-Based Educator, April's Teaching Tree, Vermont**

  As a nature-based educator, I believe in bringing in natural loose parts that have been collected around my region. Even when teaching in a small, fenced area with limited provisions, we can bring in and enhance the space by regularly bringing in natural loose parts. Ideally, staff are able to go for walks in nearby nature with the children and bring materials back to the space for play and learning.

* **Becky Gamache, Education Coordinator, Duluth Public Schools, Minnesota**

  The outdoors are filled with loose parts. Whatever catches the children's eyes and imaginations when they are outside sparks deep, rich play. The ground itself can be a dinosaur pit or a cave or a fort, depending on how the children view it and use it.

- **Cherry Mays, Early Childhood Educator, public preschool prekindergarten, Oklahoma**

  English poet William Wordsworth said, "Let Nature be your teacher." This was one of the first quotes that adorned the wall of my classroom when I began teaching prekindergarten in public school in 2004. At the time, this reflected my belief that, as beings of Nature, we are drawn to and learn from the patterns, textures, smells, tastes, and sounds of our planet. This way of learning is as old as our species. As I grew as a professional and learned more about the brain, I asked myself: Why not use those well-established neural connections to teach young children? Bring Nature into teaching.

- **Donna Mackiewicz, master naturalist and environmental educator, California**

  Living loose parts are materials from [natural items] that can be moved, carried, combined, redesigned, lined up, taken apart, and put back together in multiple ways. They can be used alone or combined with other materials. Loose parts encourage open-ended learning. There is no set of specific directions for materials that are considered loose parts. The child is the direction. Even adults can sit with no preconceived notion of doing anything then discover there is so much to see if they truly open their senses to possibilities.

- **Megan Gessler, The Morton Arboretum's Little Trees Early Learning Program, Illinois**

  I feel that children create personal knowledge and understanding by interacting with the natural world, and that includes what you are calling living loose parts. How they touch, smell, see, hear, taste, or manipulate the natural loose parts around them builds upon their deep relationship and blossoming understanding of the natural world. Every interaction builds on their biophilic connection and strengthens their kinship with the natural world.

- **Marcos Stoltzfus, Carol Good-Elliott, and Rian Bylsma, Merry Lea Environmental Learning Center, nature-based preschool and kinderforest program, Indiana**

  We see very little distinction between our loose parts options, but we do tend to encourage, rely on, and offer natural items and living loose parts. For example, while we do give empty spool reels, we more frequently give natural building blocks, pinecones, and walnut shells. We also encourage participants in some of our programs to discover their own loose parts (living or otherwise). We believe this ties in with a hyperlocal, place-based approach of "sit spots," recurring practices where children (or adults) will spend time observing and participating in the same space over the course of a day, a week, a year, or longer. We view living loose parts as a natural way to connect learners with their environment, including local loose parts.

- **Nicole Root, Founder of Playscapes, Florida**

  I used to work with children, but now I work with adults with dementia and other cognitive or physical challenges who are receiving long-term care. Because many of them are rarely able to get out and about into the real living world, I like to bring it to them. I like to think I help bring the outside in and more "life" into their day by offering them materials and objects that they would most likely not encounter otherwise.

- **Paola Lopez, Director of Kinderoo Academy, Florida**

  At its core, the concept of living loose parts in early childhood education is all about embracing natural elements and resources that foster children's creativity, imagination, and curiosity. *Living loose parts* are mainly defined to include not only plants and animals but also humans and even the living earth, such as fossils, rocks, light, and water, as manipulatives to promote observation and thinking. By incorporating living loose parts into our learning environments, our educators encourage children to engage in hands-on exploration and experimentation. Children are naturally drawn to living things and often express an innate sense of wonder and curiosity about the world around them. By providing opportunities for children to observe and interact with living things, we help nurture and sustain their sense of curiosity, leading to deeper learning and understanding.

- **Peter Dargatz, Kindergarten Teacher, Hamilton School District, Wisconsin**

  Items of nature are essential to my classroom, both inside and out. We have a nature center in the classroom with a rotating set of natural items children can observe and manipulate. Similarly, they are sure to find a treasure trove of living loose parts on our daily outdoor adventures. These items offer spontaneous curiosity that is an essential element of place-based learning.

- **Sara Evans, Early Childhood Education Nature Specialist, Green Garden Metro Detroit, Michigan**

  As a nature-oriented group of six early childhood facilities, we utilize living loose parts as a main focus of learning across our curricula. Because we are in an urban setting, there are challenges to making the spaces as close to nature as possible. But it is my personal view that immersion in nature isn't as important as exposure to as many elements as possible. The key is to provide familiarity with nature through living loose parts. We have full gardens at each site and use the steps of growing to explore, starting with seeds and then greenhouses in our lobbies, before moving plants outside, then using grown items for snack time. We even have wormeries where we put the leftovers. We also have hens at several of our locations and a Nature Explore certification.

- **Sheila Williams Ridge, Director of Child Development Laboratory School, Minnesota**

  I think of living loose parts as those things that we may engage with while learning but that also require our respect and care. To me, living loose parts are not for manipulation and our own learning but to be approached with mutuality and intention—those things we can learn from, not just learn with. In our environment we talk about seeds and the importance of a seed to a species. We don't promote experiences in which you place seeds in plastic bags for them to mold and die; instead, we think about their needs and create an environment to help the seeds flourish. We are overjoyed when we see the sprouts emerge, and we cultivate children's learning by continuing to ask questions such as, "What do you notice?" "What do you think will happen next?" and "What do you think we could do to make the seed more successful?"

- **Heather Taylor, Founder, Director, and Teacher, Outside School, California**

  [Living loose parts] are a giant part of our curriculum and a backdrop for everything we do. We're 100 percent outdoors in a regional park, so our entire classroom is alive.

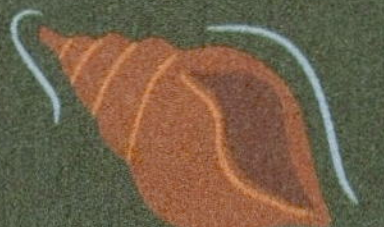

Introduction

The potential of exploring living loose parts is nearly limitless. Consider the unique aspects of your particular surroundings. Involve children in the planning and implementation of how and what living loose parts might be added into your spaces. Let the exploration begin.

How This Book Is Organized

Welcome to *Loose Parts Alive*. We start by defining living loose parts and considering why teachers incorporate them into their programs. We share strategies to explicitly teach observation skills to help children notice little details that might otherwise be overlooked in nature. We share tips for incorporating plants and animals into your day and integrating language and literacy, STEM, and social development lessons.

CHAPTER 1: LOOSE PARTS ALIVE!

The wonder of loose parts play is that it allows children to use familiar materials in innovative new ways and to ask, "What else can this be?" Open-ended loose parts play follows the children's interests. This approach to teaching and learning is fundamentally different from completing teacher-designed activities or crafts with loose parts.

By the term *living loose parts* we mean plants such as trees and flowers, animals such as pets and squirrels, as well as parts of living things such as leaves, cones, feathers, and shells. We also want to make a case for including

elements such as the living earth, light and shadow, water, fire, and wind, as well as rocks and streams. To us as teachers, it may feel risky not knowing exactly how children will engage with materials, but the payoff is worth taking a chance.

The benefits of incorporating living loose parts into our curriculum include twenty-first-century skills such as collaboration, creative thinking, communicating, flexible thinking, taking initiative, strengthening social skills, and practicing leadership. We also address ways to build biophilia and decrease biophobia in ourselves and the children we teach.

CHAPTER 2: SLOWING DOWN TO NOTICE NATURE

Today's fast-paced world can leave adults and even children stressed out and exhausted. There is calming power in nature. When we slow down and breathe deeply, we can shake off the frantic pressure to do more and instead be satisfied in doing enough. Clark (2022) recommends an unhurried approach to learning, savoring the present moment over rushing to prepare children for what's next. Slow pedagogy recognizes the collective uncertainty of the recent global pandemic years and the need for healing, promoting calm, and reducing anxiety. Our inborn sense of wonder and curiosity inspires us all to learn more about nature and the cultures around us when we slow down to discover the natural world.

CHAPTER 3: HONORING ALL LIVING THINGS

We humans feel a need to connect and communicate with other living things. We can intentionally teach respect for nature by, for example, putting spiders safely outside without killing them. Consider the example of the Texas state parks, which do not allow rocks to be moved to prevent disturbing microcosms in their ecosystem. We can help children connect to our local environments first and then expand into the larger world and introduce elements that children in our area may not otherwise encounter. Building careful observation and thoughtful reflection skills will serve children while they are in our programs and throughout their lives.

CHAPTER 4: PRACTICAL TIPS FOR INCORPORATING LIVING LOOSE PARTS

Living loose parts require special attention, care, and logistics. From lending libraries to caring for animals to getting parents on board to figuring out outdoor toileting, plan for the practical side of this approach. Additionally, children can share in the responsibility of watering plants and feeding animals. When we gather natural materials with children, we can teach them to notice where they were collected and return them later.

CHAPTER 5: PLAYING IT SAFE: DEATH, DECAY, AND REASONABLE RISK

Interacting with the natural world inherently includes risky play. Consider policies around stick play, working with fire, and how to conduct a benefit-risk analysis in your space. Additionally, explore the concepts of death, decay, and decomposition. As death is a natural part of life, how do we notice and talk about the cycle of life around us in our settings?

CHAPTER 6: CREATIVE THINKING AND TECHNOLOGY SPRINGBOARDS

Living loose parts naturally inspire creative thinking. We can start with the familiar materials already around us to create place-based, personal, and cultural connections. Exploring in natural settings has also been linked to greater self-esteem and reduced stress (Melson, 2013). As teachers, we have almost unlimited options in setting up our environments, asking questions, and offering props and ideas to extend children's creative thinking.

CHAPTER 7: ASKING GOOD QUESTIONS, ASSESSING LEARNING

Living loose parts promote curiosity when we set the stage for unfamiliar or unexpected events to pique children's interest. As teachers, we can plan *discrepant events*—surprising or unexpected outcomes—which act as an invitation for children to ask their own investigative questions, perhaps with plants, ants, worms, or goldfish, as we teach observation skills. We can assess children's learning through authentic assessment using checklists, notes, recordings, photos, and conversations with the children. This data is useful in lesson planning and can be shared with stakeholders through parent conferences and progress reports.

CHAPTER 8: BRANCHING OUT WITH STEM

Children create working theories about how things work. Through play, they test those theories: "How many rocks will fit in my pockets?" "I wonder if I can catch that butterfly." *Praxis* is literally putting our theories into practice. Science, technology, engineering, and math make exploring nature and the natural world possible. Children explore habitats and create classifications, such as things with wings and things with scales, using science. They measure, count, group, and compare with mathematics and use engineering to create architecture and solve problems. Using high-tech tools, such as digital cameras and tablet computers, and low-tech tools, such as pencils and sticks, they are making and testing working theories. When we provide open-ended materials and supportive attention, we are helping children build sturdy foundations for all their later learning.

CHAPTER 9: GETTING DRAMATIC WITH LIVING LOOSE PARTS

Living loose parts enhance language fluency by giving children something real and meaningful to talk about. Their excitement about learning bubbles up in conversations with you, their friends, and their families. Oral language inspirations include living things as well as representations such as puppets, drawings, and flannelboard story retelling. Written language invitations might include journaling, observing and recording, and storymaking. Research continues to show that children use more expressive language and more creative storylines in their play when the props they use are less specific and more representative. For example, the Timpani toy study (Measimer, 2015) found children with a highly detailed cash register that made sounds focused on pushing the buttons and making the sounds. But children with a wooden block in the general shape of a cash register pretended to be shoppers and clerks and used the vocabulary associated with a store. In playgrounds that use natural materials rather than concrete, plastic, and metal, young children's play becomes more creative and imaginative.

CHAPTER 10: LIVING LOOSE pARTS

The arts include expressing ideas through movement, music, visual arts, and simple props and costumes. Artistic representations of the natural world help us understand living things in new ways. When children express their ideas through clay, paint, crayons, or markers, they can show us exactly what they are thinking. When they use cameras or tablets to record their work in still and video photography, they can show as well as tell the world what they are learning. Music, movement, and dance allow children to use their whole bodies to express their ideas. The process of creating art provides a natural opportunity to connect across generations as we express ideas, memories, hopes, and dreams.

CHAPTER 11: SUPPORTING FEELINGS AND FRIENDSHIP

Living things provide opportunities to teach empathy by caring for living plants and animals as well as classmates. Children can imagine an animal's perspective through pretend play with their own bodies, costumes, and props. Animal puppets and realistic play figures allow children to take on animal personas and play out different points of view. Friendship skills can be explicitly taught at each child's level of understanding with picture books and stories and can be supported with observation and suggestions. Getting to know the children and families in our program will help us understand when a child is overstressed. We can help children become more aware of their own feelings and can teach breathing and other calm-down methods before children become overly upset. We can foster social-emotional development through positive expectations, creating and enforcing rules together, and building a sense of belonging and a community of caring for one another.

As we, the authors, visit programs around the United States and the world, we are in awe of the creative energy and amazing ideas we see educators and young children put into practice every day. We want to amplify voices from the field and honor their work by sharing their stories, along with our own experiences, throughout this book. We hope they inspire you to think of something you've never thought of before and to find joy wherever you are in your journey.

CHAPTER 1

Loose Parts Alive!

"Those who contemplate the beauty of the earth find reserves of strength that will endure as long as life lasts."

—Rachel Carson, environmentalist and author

Loose parts are moveable, adaptable objects to be used in a variety of ways in open-ended play. Imagine loose parts not just as a collection of objects in a pile, bin, or basket but also as living plants, animals, and even our own bodies. These living loose parts, by just being alive, capture a child's interest. Children will want to observe and investigate to find out more about them. To build on this intrinsic motivation for discovery, let's explore living loose parts as a catalyst for creative ideas, an invitation to curiosity through STEM, artistic expression, and authentic opportunities to build language fluency.

Because loose parts play without the child is just a pile of stuff, at its core, the approach relies on the child to invent ideas and test hypotheses—to authentically play. In this way, loose parts play becomes therapeutic. Children aren't waiting on adults to tell them what to do or guess the right answer that an adult has in mind. They are learning to listen to and trust their own inner voice. In the words of Eleanor Duckworth, professor emerita at the Harvard Graduate School of Education, they are experiencing "the having of wonderful ideas." Supportive adults observe this self-directed play and may ask questions to clarify a child's current understanding or make suggestions to extend children's thinking. The role of the adult is primarily to set up inviting environments and then to sit back and watch, to trust the child and to observe the social and academic growth in not-so-academic-looking settings. Natural materials and outdoor surroundings also provide calming comfort from nature. When anxiety is lowered, children learn more efficiently. This is true for typically developing children and especially true for children with sensory defensiveness and issues with impulse control, including those on the autism spectrum.

Welcome to a Living Loose Parts Journey

Whether you've been incorporating loose parts into your work for decades or are just becoming curious, we thank you for your work and dedication. Let's begin by focusing on young children's curiosity:

"Does this rose rock need to be watered?"

"Do mermaids make the rocks shiny when the creek splashes on them?"

If we can overcome our impulse to provide quick and ready answers for young children and instead begin to embrace these questions as they are lived, we will grow natural researchers and scientists organically in our classrooms. We can reimagine our own environments to promote children's thinking through living loose parts and the natural world.

In response to the rose rock question, after his teacher reassured him that no, it was a rock and didn't need watering, the four-year-old child decided that he would still water it "just in case." The preschool class that wondered about mermaids working in their creek decided to start an investigation. With their teacher's support, they gathered supplies, including shiny sequins (mermaid scales). During the planning phase of this research project, one child said, "We also need a sun committee, because wet rocks also need sunshine to look shiny." Easy answers are not the most efficient way to learn. When children discover their own answers, even in recursive, nonlinear ways, the resulting information is learned more deeply and is more easily applied to new situations. We must learn to trust children to discover their own learning pathways because, as psychologist Jean Piaget, put it, "Children have real understanding only of that which they invent themselves, and each time that we try to teach them something too quickly, we keep them from reinventing it themselves" (quoted in Papert, 1999). And more recently in the words of Terry Doyle, author of *Learner-Centered Teaching: Putting the Research on Learning into Practice* (2011): "Whoever does the work does the learning."

Biophilia vs. Biophobia

There is extensive research around the benefits to children of being outside in nature; yet, many children suffer from *biophobia*, or fear of the outdoors. According to Melson (2013), children could not identify a handful of local flora or fauna; however, they correctly identified more than a thousand corporate logos. Fortunately, exposure and playful, investigative time spent outdoors can help build *biophilia*, or the natural affinity to the living world.

Biophilia can grow bit by bit when we allow hesitant children to observe from afar. Acknowledging, "It's okay if you watch from over there," will help children become more comfortable. We can scaffold explorations by

offering food handlers' gloves, tongs, sticks, or chopsticks to children until they are ready to touch things with their fingers or hands. We can model open curiosity about living things with our words and actions. Children gain confidence when they see other children playing and having fun. Laughter is a powerful anxiety reducer.

Childhood is a crux at which it is essential to help children develop a love of nature. Through interacting with the living world, they can build their capacities for problem solving, critical thinking, and divergent thinking to come up with better solutions for the damage caused by our human impact on this living planet. While we don't need to burden children with the weight of responsibility for Earth's future, we can facilitate playful and joyful encounters with living loose parts that naturally help them become good stewards. "Just as we help children to develop an ethic of caring for one another, we can encourage children to expand this ethic to include other species and the ecologies all depend upon for survival" (Melson, 2013).

Children themselves may not be changing, but with the explosion in the availability of smartphones and tablets over the past two decades, childhood is changing. Either out of concern for safety or lack of time for supervision, parents report that their children are spending less time outdoors than the parents did as children. A study from the United Kingdom found that 83 percent of children between the ages of five and sixteen weren't able to identify a bumblebee. "Out of 1,000 children shown pictures of native plants and animals, 82% did not recognize an oak leaf and nearly five out of 10 failed to spot a bluebell" (World Economic Forum, 2019).

We can help reconnect children with our natural surroundings by encouraging them to notice and draw or photograph the nature that surrounds us. By asking, "What does that make you think of?" we encourage them to connect memories and strengthen their neural pathways by reinforcing connections and creating categories. A logical next step is then to ask them to write or add a caption to their drawing or scribble. We can revisit these nature journals over time to see how their thoughts are changing and notice how children's ideas are becoming more complex as the year progresses.

> Heartland Montessori program's back door opens onto a parking lot. The educators decided to fence an area of asphalt and bring in piles of sticks, rocks, and leaves. They found children sequencing the sticks like the Red Rod meter sticks. They were replaying their math lessons with the natural materials.
>
> —Charlotte Wood-Wilson

When children have room to learn more about our natural world, the time they spend in nature can make an impact on mental and physical health as well. An article in *Time* (Sifferlin, 2016) addresses the benefits of time spent in nature, asserting that it:

- increases awe,
- alleviates symptoms of depression and anxiety,
- decreases the symptoms of attention-deficit and hyperactivity disorder (ADHD),
- decreases blood pressure,
- promotes cancer-fighting cells, and
- improves mental health.

Connecting to nature offers these benefits for us as educators, too! This journey has a place for everyone. There is room for those of us with access to acres of nature as well as for those who notice nature growing in flowerpots, on rooftop gardens, and in sidewalk cracks.

A More Expansive View of Loose Parts

Given what we are learning about the benefits that nature offers, what if we expand our definition of loose parts to include living things, such as plants, animals, or even our own bodies? Join us on a journey to explore the concept of living loose parts in the context of STEM, creative thinking, curiosity, the arts, and language fluency.

As educators working with loose parts, we have heard lots of "rules."

"You can't paint it, or it's not a loose part."

"We're getting rid of plastics so we can do loose parts."

"Toys can't be loose parts."

It seems many of these rules have been put around loose parts that aren't in the original theory by Simon Nicholson (1971) and may place limits on our current understanding of the children in our settings. Nicholson equated loose parts with variables in a setting: "In any environment, both the degree of inventiveness and creativity, and the possibility of discovery, are directly proportional to the number and kind of variables in it" (1970).

How do you define loose parts? Has that understanding changed over time? Come back to this concept at the end of the book and as you continue to experiment and explore the great world around us. If you are a novice to the concept of loose parts, getting started can be quite easy, though you'll find endless options to explore in time. In a *Loose Parts Nature Play* podcast episode on getting started with loose parts, Carla suggests the following:

- Recognize it is already happening!
- Play! Start playing with some items and see how else they may be used.
- Start with what you already have on hand.
- Let go of your need for control and let it happen.
- Start with a book or prompt, then get out of the way.
- Study the children. What are their interests, curiosities, and ideas?
- Be responsive to their inquisitiveness by pairing their ideas with an invitation to explore loose parts.

- Start with *schema*, a term Piaget used to describe our brain's universal structures for interpreting sensory information. Today, the term is used as shorthand for *schematic play*, or repeated behaviors used to explore the world around us (Forman and Kuschner, 1983). Have loose parts freely available for children for experimentation and exploration.

- Involve children!

- Study and read (and listen) about loose parts. Exchange articles, professional development books, and so on, with other educators.

- Network. Create or join a loose parts play group.

Once you've played around with the basics a bit, expanding to living loose parts can be a transformative step. Nicholson hinted at the concept of living loose parts when he expanded loose parts to variables and phenomena outside of small wooden objects, such as blocks:

> There is evidence that all children love to interact with variables, such as materials and shapes; smells and other physical phenomena, such as electricity, magnetism and gravity; media such as gases and fluids; sounds, music and motion; chemical interactions, cooking and fire, and other people, and animals, plants, words, concepts and ideas. With all these things all children love to play, experiment, discover and invent and have fun. All these things have one thing in common, which is variables or "loose parts" (Nicholson, 1971).

So many aspects of the living world can become part of our loose parts play. Additionally, widening the definition sets the stage for experimentation and exploration of variables as the standard of what loose parts are. "Whether there are seasonal changes to note, animals and insects to study, or gardens to be tended to—nature is the best teacher!" (Monsalvatge, Long, and DiBello, 2013).

Carla and her colleagues specifically looked at loose parts in outdoor classrooms as part of one study. They observed, "It is curious to note the inclusion of living things, children's own bodies, and roly-poly bugs as loose parts. Ultimately, the way these are used can be moveable variables in the environment" (Gull, Bogunovich, Goldstein, and Rosengarten, 2019). As they listed what can be found in outdoor settings, they realized that these were living loose parts. They also were surprised to find that some options in the overall environment, such as a low brick wall, that may not traditionally be considered loose parts were open-ended variables when approached with a loose parts mindset. They recorded more than twenty-three plants or plant parts in the outdoor classrooms. "Living plants seem to be the most useful when it comes to play because they create things such as pinecones, acorns, and leaves. This type of environment allows children to use the dirt, sand, grass, mulch, and ground to transform the environment into something different. The next most-used materials were parts of the trees, such as twigs, branches, logs, bark, and stumps" (Gull, Bogunovich, Goldstein, and Rosengarten, 2019).

Nature itself is a large living variable. In the settings with outdoor classrooms, children preferred natural loose parts: "sticks, logs, snow, and sand can be repurposed into anything that a child wants these to be" (Gull,

Bogunovich, Goldstein, and Rosengarten, 2019). All are part of earthly processes and often are teeming with life. In one outdoor classroom setting, children were given opportunities to explore a frozen pumpkin or snow and to discover how they can become ingredients in recipes (Kiewra and Veselack, 2016). In the ever-changing environment, children were able to problem solve, think creatively, and have flexible concepts as they adjusted their observations and learning on a regular basis.

In their research, Carla and her colleagues came up with a definition of loose parts.

> Loose parts are open-ended, interactive, natural, and manufactured materials that can be manipulated with limitless possibilities. Interaction with loose parts includes experimentation, exploration, and playful interactions with variables through creativity and imagination. Participants have the freedom to explore variables, combine materials, and react to complex ideas and themes that emerge. Facilitators encourage participants, make loose parts available, stimulate discovery, provide opportunities, allow for open-ended play, and prompt meaningful connections and experiences. Through loose parts explorations, participants develop imagination, creativity, and collaborative skills. Process is more important than the end product, fostering overall growth and development (Gull, Bogunovich, Goldstein, and Rosengarten, 2019).

Plants and animals are among the first things we think of in the category of living loose parts. They fascinate children and provide endless opportunities for play, learning, and engagement. Plants even make their own food—how cool is that? They transform energy from the sun into their nourishment. We can cultivate those plants for special purposes such as changing the landscape, eating, and building. You may already plant gardens outdoors and bring plants into the classroom to add life to learning spaces. Along with living plants, we can explore their leaves, needles, seeds, cones, sticks, and flowers. Suspected allergens can be sealed in bags or jars for safer investigations.

Animal encounters can take many forms in learning settings, from classroom pets to visiting zoo ambassador animals or the slug the children found under a log in our outdoor classroom.

As humans, we often think of animals existing outside of ourselves; however, as children often remind us, humans are animals too. Our bodies are living loose parts that interpret, explore, and experiment. Children can combine and move their bodies into letter or number shapes as living loose parts that build literacy, big body coordination, and spatial skills. When our bodies are introduced as shadow makers, we've embraced living loose parts. Dance, the language of human bodies in motion, expresses stories, emotions, and grace. Not only are we alive, but we are also a part of nature. We are nature, just as the plants and other animals around us are part of the natural world.

Shadows may not be *living* loose parts, but many kinds of shadow makers are. As illustrated in the video *Shadow Stories* (North American Reggio Alliance, 2012), the sun's journey across the sky causes shadows to move, sometimes faster than the children can trace them onto butcher paper. The almost magical properties of an overhead projector combined with a collection of objects that block the light, causing shadows, can promote a sense of wonder and awe during playful exploration with these phenomena. In a similar vein, tracing the edge of a puddle on a sidewalk with chalk, then returning periodically on a sunny day, gives children an opportunity to notice evaporation in real time: "What's happening here?" If we invite them to share their ideas of what is causing the changes to the size and shape of the puddle under the hot sun, we teach young children to be curious about the natural world. If we do not correct their approximations of understanding, but instead honor their ideas, we are teaching young children to trust their own thinking.

"Are trees sad when they lose their leaf friends in the fall?"

–Three-year-old child

"Do wire birds need breakfast?"

–Two-year-old child

The Earth is alive with dynamic systems such as volcanoes, hurricanes, and moving glaciers. Likewise, healthy soil is alive with microorganisms: fungi, bacteria, arthropods, insects, and protozoa that help break down materials to provide nutrients to plants. The active process of decomposition of organic matter is very much alive. Even a dead animal is full of invertebrates and bacteria changing the structure of the matter. While it may be kind of gross to consider a dead animal as a living thing, we can also promote a sense of wonder that the earth can recycle matter and waste on its own: the circle of life. As Rachel Carson (1956) observes, "The lasting pleasures of contact with the natural world are not reserved for scientists but are available to anyone who will place himself under the influence of earth, sea, and sky and their amazing life." All of us, from babies to elders, can explore the living loose parts that the earth graciously provides.

LIVING LOOSE PARTS WITH INFANTS AND TODDLERS

The more time we spend in the company of people under three, the better we appreciate the scope of information they are processing, despite such a short time on Earth. Our youngest citizens discover details of living creatures and plants, revealing their complex thoughts and capabilities through digital photos they take and in their own words and expressions. Respectful early care professionals document children's thinking and strive to create calm, joy-filled creative environments where very young children and their caregivers want to spend time together learning about the natural world. From the three-year-old child's theories about changes to the playground trees in the autumn to the two-year-old's playful concern for "hungry" toys to the multiage class's daily investigations of ants in the dirt, we can embrace loose parts play with respectful interactions with living things. This allows us to observe complex ideas expressed through young children's language and play.

Elinor Goldschmied, an educator who worked with infants and toddlers, embraced the idea of loose parts play through her pioneering work with the concepts of heuristic, or discovery, play: treasure baskets for babies and islands of discovery for toddlers. A treasure basket is a low, sturdy basket filled with items from nature or around the house. Babies find these interesting because of the variety in appearance, including textures, smells, surface temperatures, weight, and the sounds they can make. Plastic toys, on the other hand, tend to have similar smells, temperature, and taste, which make them boring by comparison. Islands of discovery are the next logical step. As babies begin to crawl and toddle, they are constantly on the move. Islands of discovery can be blankets, mats, baskets, or buckets of materials placed around the room or playground to allow young children to explore objects while also honoring their need to be in motion. As added enticements, Goldschmied suggested adding surprises, such as a large crystal hidden inside a zipped bag or a string of beads in a small basket, as treasures to be discovered during the child's exploration (Wilhelm, 2017).

BABIES, LET'S GO OUTSIDE!

No one earns more respect than those who care for our youngest citizens. It is deeply rewarding, yet physically and mentally exhausting work to anticipate and provide for a roomful of tiny humans' physical, emotional, and learning needs. All at once. All day long. Every. Day. Getting outdoors is a healthy choice and is calming and refreshing for babies and adults alike, but programs need to plan support to make this easier to do in the baby rooms and any rooms with non-mobile children. The responsibility to figure out the logistics shouldn't rest on the shoulders of the infant/toddler teachers alone. This might involve switching rooms so these classes can directly access the playground and arranging the staff schedule to include extra hands during the day to make sure there are enough people to transport babies outside and to respond to everyone's sleeping, diapering, and toileting needs while some staff are outdoors. When designing buildings, include transitional spaces such as covered porches and patios so children have options to play indoors, outdoors, and in between. Consider sliding or overhead doors and ramps instead of steps to make it easier to get classes outside and back in again. In warmer climates, add fast-growing trees or large shades to protect babies' delicate skin from direct sunlight. Remove any hazards, including toxic plants and anything that poses a risk of choking, such as pea gravel and acorns. We know babies learn by putting things in their mouths. We need to provide opportunities for safe exploration and to sanitize larger items between uses.

PLACE-BASED EDUCATION

Children need direct, firsthand observational experiences. In early childhood, we can begin with a focus on local animals and habitats that are part of a child's everyday environment rather than exotic animals, rainforests, arctic areas, or the ocean (unless they are part of your local ecosystem). Once children form connections with the animals in their own backyard, sidewalks, and playground, you may choose to begin introducing animals that they may not encounter naturally each day, especially through realistic encounters: live animal webcams and zoo or aquarium visits. Have conversations that help children connect the new plants and animals with the more familiar local varieties. This is especially important for children who may not have opportunities to travel outside their neighborhoods very often. A wider range of experiences builds children's knowledge and vocabulary related to those plants and animals.

Consider where children are currently finding information about animals and the natural world. Shows, books, films, and games such as the PBS series *Wild Kratts*, *Finding Nemo*, YouTube videos, the Pete the Cat series, *The Pokey Little Puppy*, or The Sneaky Snacky Squirrel do not offer realistic portrayals of animal behavior. Some children absorb attitudes from their family members or have direct pet experiences; others only see adult reactions to nature in their schools. What messages about the living world are we sending? Do our intentions match the messages children are receiving? How can we provide opportunities that allow children to create their own unique bonds with nature around them?

David Sobel (1996) advocates for a place-based education, learning about what is right around us. He advises:

> From ages four to seven, children's homes fill the center of their maps, and much of their play is within sight or earshot of the home. Children often describe the worms, chipmunks, and pigeons that live in their yards or on their blocks, and they feel protective of these creatures.

> We should be attempting to engage children more deeply in knowing the flora, fauna, and character of their own local places. The woods behind the school and the neighborhood streets and stores are the places to start.

Living animals typically trump anything else we educators can bring into the classroom. Children notice the chipmunk at the window outside, are intrigued by the worm they find while digging, and are enthralled when a live animal is brought into the classroom. They are wired to investigate other living things in their environments. How are they the same and different? What is unique about this organism? How does it survive?

As we journey through the concept of living loose parts, we will share ideas, examples, "starts" (but never-ending points), and inspiration. Please note that this concept will never quite be done; it will continually evolve as we explore and experiment with the variables in our environment. How does exploring living loose parts apply to your setting and space with the unique children in your care? What is special about the living things in your area to explore?

Using nature that we find in our space is a great approach to living loose parts, as illustrated by the following examples and uses of loose parts found at Merry Lea Environmental Learning Center of Goshen College in Indiana.

- Ice is a loose part that we use most cold days in some way. Since we are located in northern Indiana, we can anticipate having ice for a significant part of the school year (though this is shifting with climate change). Since the path to our outdoor classroom leads next to a pond and a wetland, students are quick to notice when ice begins to form and it always inspires curiosity and engagement. We help students learn how to judge the safety of ice as soon as ice starts to form. We allow them to explore the many different sounds ice makes—tossing pebbles onto the surface, sliding pebbles across the surface, tapping on the ice with sticks, etc. Students also have the chance to test and experiment with the thickness of ice—using sticks to try to break it, tossing stones onto the surface to see if the ice supports the stones, breaking the ice by kicking it with their boot heels while sitting on the ground beside the wetland, eventually going onto the ice themselves when it is safe to do so. Students have worked as groups to lift large plates of ice from the wetland after breaking the ice at the edge; they have built structures with the ice pieces; and they have used ice pieces to create games such as seeing how far they can slide ice pieces across the surface of the remaining ice. They have painted ice, encased other living loose parts in ice, discovered ice growing inside other living loose parts, and discovered ice in many surprising places. Students are also noticing that ice doesn't form at the same rate, thickness, and so on, across all the water places they encounter each day, leading to wonderings about why this is so.

- Walnuts, which fall every year onto the trail to our outdoor classroom and in our classroom, are used in many ways:
    - Comparing sizes
    - Comparing shapes

    - Comparing the number, sizes, and shapes of holes chewed in them
    - Peeling/breaking off the husk to find what is inside
    - Discovering and learning about the larvae that feed on the inner part of the husks
    - Putting the husk pieces in water to make dye/ink/paint
    - Rubbing the husk pieces on paper to make designs
    - Breaking open the hard shells—experimenting with the use of rocks, hammers, and other tools to see what works to crack the shells
    - Discovering where the walnut fruits are coming from and where they were growing before falling

- Water is constantly combined with other loose parts, even when it isn't frozen. It is used for mixing, sorting, floating and sinking, painting, changing how slippery other parts are, and more. We use the roof of a small shelter to fill a rain barrel and investigate how even small amounts of water will change.

Loose parts may be purchased, but they can also be found in nature. While nothing in nature should be taken for granted, sticks, sand, soil, pinecones, and leaves may be borrowed and returned to nature at little cost. Children can smell the flowers and plants and observe and even photograph some animals without disrupting them. Later, children can review the pictures, discuss observations, and make representations on paper or with clay to revisit and extend children's thinking.

As we more fully embrace the what and why of living loose parts, we start thinking of the logistics and how to notice and encourage respectful interaction with living loose parts in our settings. As we slow down and observe what is around us, we find infinite possibilities for learning and play.

In the next chapter, we explore ways to provide interactions with living loose parts. We make a case for slow pedagogy: slowing down to savor and digest learning, rather than frantically trying to cram in as much information as possible into our lessons. Slowing down helps children make sense of what they are learning and can serve as an antidote to the stress of an otherwise fast-paced world.

CHAPTER 2

Slowing Down to Notice Nature

With so much learning to discover, you may be wondering, "How do I get started?"

Some people are comfortable diving in with both feet, while others only want to dip a toe in the water. Either approach works just fine with living loose parts. You may already be doing more than you realize. As you prepare to do more, think about where you can enlist help and support. See if you can build a community of practice with your co-workers, the families you serve, or friends with similar interests.

Slowing Down to Notice

Children are naturally inquisitive about the world around them; however, some of us may shut that curiosity down as we encounter resistance from adults and society around us. We can give children permission (which is actually a child's right) to just be in our natural spaces and get curious. Tools can help as we open our spaces for curious children. Let's explore a few options as tools for curiosity.

SIT SPOTS

A sit spot is simply a place outside where a person can regularly spend a short time (usually five to fifteen minutes, starting at one or two minutes and gradually getting longer as children develop skills) in the same spot. Returning to the same spot daily, weekly, monthly, or quarterly allows us to be still and consider what is around us. This sensory practice allows the participant to notice the intricacies of nature around us: the colors, sounds, textures, smells, and more! Sit spots allow for "self-exploration, to develop a sense of self-awareness and an appreciation for a student's own space" (Merry Lea Environmental Learning Center, n.d.). During this time, children may examine nearby sticks or natural loose parts, observe an insect, create patterns or artwork, or look up at the sky. After the sit spot time, participants gather and share what they noticed and are curious about with the group.

To set up for sit spots, students should be able to choose their own space within the designated area that educators can see. While a more natural space is preferred, this can happen in any space (which might include looking out the window), considering where nature may be in our environment. The teacher can make a map to help children remember where their spot is as routines are built. A small yoga mat or foam flooring square can give the child a place to sit and insulate from the ground a bit. A notebook allows the child to draw, journal, and record observations. While sit spot time is short, it allows the participant to slow down, focus, and observe what is important to them at the moment. Tools such as magnifying glasses, mirrors, small shovels, or guidebooks may be available from time to time. Children can visit these spaces in all kinds of weather to get to know the local seasons.

"In our busy world, these times are not only precious, but necessary."
(Fravel, 2017)

> Our sit spot practice encourages the engagement with the "living" part of living loose parts within a place-based experience. The space used for sit spots contains many loose parts (since our sit spots tend to be in natural settings) and these spaces, including the loose parts within them, change over time. Ice forms and melts, ephemeral flowers appear in the spring, leaves fall and decay, a repetitive activity such as drumming on a log marks or wears away loose parts. Animals moving through the space bring in and remove loose parts. Our learners will also modify sit spots as they move about with other activities in our classroom at Merry Lea Environmental Learning Center.

Exploring Loose Parts with Live Plants

Just as animals offer invigorating observations, plants are pleasing to the senses, versatile, and intriguing. Caring for plants helps children learn responsibility and develop a sense of accomplishment. Adding more indoor and outdoor plants to your setting will offer opportunities for the children to slow down and notice as plants grow, change, and attract insects and wildlife.

Living plants in the classroom provide children with the opportunity to learn responsibility. Checking on plants can be a child's job each day. Watering with a spray bottle or by placing a drinking straw in a cup of water and covering the top with a fingertip then releasing the water into the pot by moving your finger away are two ways to help prevent overwatering. Children can use rulers to measure plant growth periodically and record their findings in a plant journal. This also provides an authentic purpose for measuring, reading, and writing. They can inspect plant leaves, especially the undersides, for pests with a magnifying glass, and treat infestations with soapy water. Apps such as iNaturalist can help you identify plants, and Seed to Spoon can help you plan indoor and outdoor gardening projects. Several studies (Lee et al., 2015; Mason et al., 2022) have found that plants in the classroom and on the school grounds, and even pictures of plants, help us feel calmer. Gardening provides opportunities for children to learn to safely use tools like rakes and shovels, get their hands dirty in living soil, and observe changes as plants grow. We've found that children are more willing to try new foods they've grown themselves.

Angela Haupt (2023) reported in *Time* that when a person is repotting a plant, their blood pressure is reduced. Children can concentrate better in a classroom with live plants, but even fake plants and posters of plants have positive effects (Lee et al., 2015; Mason et al., 2022).

Using native plants is always a win, but other garden and ornamental plants can add variety. Try to entice all the senses as part of our plant offerings. Teach children to cup their hands around herbs and flowers to smell the scent without damaging the plant.

Not sure where to start? Please check with local master gardeners or landscapers for details on your growing zone and appropriate plants for your space. Some plant suggestions to consider for your spaces are included below, but try to incorporate native, local plants in your settings as much as possible.

There are many ways to introduce plants into your classroom. First, make sure that the plants you choose are nontoxic. Good sources for checking include your local county extension office and poison control (www.poison.org), which includes photographs of poisonous plants. Safe and beautiful potted plants that you might choose include African violet, Swedish ivy, spider plants (also called airplane plants), and Christmas cactus.

Outdoors, native plants for your area will grow deeper roots and are more likely to survive local weather conditions. You may want to create a sensory garden that appeals to the five senses. For bright visual appeal, consider lantana, yarrow, red osier, and vegetables in the colors of the rainbow. Lemon balm, lavender, lilac, spicebush, and hyacinth produce heady scents. Interesting textures of lamb's ear, river birch, and bluestar are inviting to touch. Plants that rustle, such as money trees and switchgrass, and those that rattle, such as lotus seed pods, make interesting sounds. Children can taste honeysuckle, strawberries, herbs, and berries. Herbs grow quickly and can be added to lunch; consider basil, mint, chives, sage, and dill. You may want to grow them in raised beds or containers because sometimes they really spread. You can appeal to the sense of proprioception and children's sense of accomplishment through heavy work by giving them opportunities to move logs, bags of soil, and flowerpots.

"We focus on loose parts that are present in our ecosystem in Minnesota, like pinecones, cattails, milkweed pods, pine needles, rocks, snow, leaves, and so on."

–Sheila Williams Ridge

We often think of springtime for gardening lessons, but some plants do well in every season. In the winter, kale, broccoli, cabbage, and radishes will grow, even under snow. Pumpkins, carrots, and wildflowers planted in late summer will be ready for harvest in the fall. Midsummer crops include garlic, onions, potatoes, and cabbage. Spring plants include lettuce, peas, and tomatoes. You can start them indoors and move them outside after the last threat of frost.

Fast-growing trees and shrubs can provide playground shade in just a few years. Chinese elm is a sturdy, fast-growing shade tree that tolerates urban conditions. Boxwood makes a great barrier for balls. Some people find succulents, such as aloe and hens and chicks, easy to grow. Consider planting bamboo in containers, as it tends to spread and can become invasive. Willow bends easily, so it works well for growing shade tunnels and play huts. Willow sticks are great for creating playhouses.

Another setting explored plants more intentionally by creating a pizza garden that infiltrated dramatic play, science, and math investigations.

> A local farmer donated supplies for us to grow a "pizza garden" at our Montessori preschool. The children cultivated the soil, planted the seeds, watered, and weeded. We sprayed only soap and water as pesticide. A visitor from the National Agriculture in the Classroom program commented, "This is their garden, not yours. I can tell because the rows aren't straight, the seeds look like they were planted by the handful, and the children have stepped on some of the plants. That's how it should be."
>
> We have found children are more likely to try things like banana peppers when they pick them right off the vine. Sometimes, parents say, "My child doesn't like that," but the child finds that they actually do. Gardening [informs] the children's dramatic play. They pretend to buy and sell produce, shovel to turn over soil in the compost pile, and turn compost in the sandbox. We found children suddenly bringing more vegetables in their lunchboxes. When we grew giant sunflowers, we thought birds were scattering their seeds on our sidewalk until a child noticed a little mouse scaling a stem to reach the seed head five or six feet in the air. Because we don't use pesticides, we have more insects, birds, mice, and squirrels to observe. We wrote messages of peace on strips of cloth at the back of our garden to blow in the wind.
>
> —Charlotte Wood-Wilson

If your program is not in an area with expansive natural areas, you can still explore nature. Urban settings may feel like nothing but concrete; however, you can intentionally discover and enhance nature right where you are. Look in sidewalk cracks, vacant lots, and nearby green spaces; you will find nature all around. Take a walk to explore what your spaces have to offer. Use online maps to help "find" green areas to explore on your adventures. Reach out to a local "yardener," or person who is growing plants and produce in their yard, to ask to bring the children for short neighborhood visits. Most will want to share their love of plants and ecosystems.

If your only outdoor space is on a balcony or rooftop, you can still garden with children. Most flowers and vegetables can be grown in pots. Children will love watering them with watering cans or a hose, and overwatering is less of a problem in hot weather. Planting milkweed, coneflower, zinnias, and lantana will attract butterflies. Lavender, milkweed, and marigolds also attract moths. Ladybugs, which can be purchased at garden supply stores, will eat pesky aphids. These beneficial insects are attracted to dill, cilantro, marigolds, and yarrow. Providing a shallow dish of water and places to hide may attract lizards to your urban garden, even if it's on a balcony or roof. There might even be insect larvae in shallow standing water.

"The hand is the instrument of intelligence. The child needs to manipulate objects and to gain experience by touching and handling."

—Maria Montessori, ***The 1946 London Lectures***

Nature is everywhere, not just in parks and preserves but also in the sidewalk cracks where sand or soil and weeds appear. Sidewalk cracks are good places to investigate sand, soil, clay, mud, and living plants such as grass, dandelions, or henbit. Back or front yards often have grassy patches or wildflowers, squirrels, birds, as well as loose parts such as rocks, sticks, dirt, and clay. Parks and vacant lots may provide habitat for moths, butterflies, frogs, and toads, and other critters. In the park, notice trees and shrubs, grasshoppers, ladybugs, and worms. Get to know the plants by the seasons in these precious spaces using apps such as iNaturalist.

Books for Exploring Nature in Urban Settings

Guillain, Charlotte. 2017. *The Street Beneath My Feet*. London, UK: words & pictures.

Malnor, Carol L. 2016. *Wild Ones: Observing City Critters*. Nevada City, CA: Dawn Publications.

Walmsley, Naomi. 2020. *Urban Forest School: Outdoor Adventures and Skills for City Kids*. Lewes, UK: GMC Publications.

Evaluating Your Space

To include living loose parts and more nature in your program, you might want to start small. Consider your space. What natural affordances are provided? What can you add or change?

- Create a digging area outside where children can discover grubs, pill bugs, worms, and other critters in the soil.
- Add tools such as magnifying glasses, bug jars, scoop nets, viewing habitats, and binoculars.
- Provide photo cards and handy reference guides or identification apps on a tablet to build children's interest in the rocks, bugs, and plants they find. As they learn names and descriptions of the living things they discover, they will also build their vocabulary and opportunities to practice verbal language fluency.
- Buy worms or crickets at the pet store or a local bait shop to bring into the class for short observations.
- Plant a garden! Critters will be built in.
- Make a chart of animals spotted in your space. Post it in the classroom or hallway and add to it throughout the year.
- Invite families to add to another chart or to your website the things they spot at home or on their travels.
- Add digital photos and revisit the growing list as a class to compare what's alike and different about the entries.
- Notice how seasonal changes impact the bugs and plants you see around the school.

WILD WOODS

Slowing Down for Curiosity

The old saying, "Curiosity killed the cat," was meant to curb inquisitiveness, a sort of "mind ya business" approach to life. Many of us may have memories of being discouraged from asking so many questions as children and perhaps from taking chances as adults. Do you view curiosity as a good thing or a bad thing? Your authors—former curious kids who grew into teachers, professors, and mothers—believe a curious approach to life is a positive thing. Reading a wide variety of materials, listening to blogs, watching documentaries, and striking up conversations with strangers and friends make our lives more interesting. Our curious approach to life leads us to challenge our students and our own children to think more creatively. We want to live in a world where people are curious lifelong learners. Perhaps we could update that old saying. We could say instead, that curiosity *skilled* or *filled* or *thrilled* the cat. In this kind of wordplay, the words themselves become loose parts to be explored in our minds and on paper. Curiosity is the internal state or disposition that leads to the act of creativity.

Kashdan (2018) found curiosity could be motivated by five factors:

- Joyous exploration: curiosity for the joy of discovery
- Deprivation sensitivity: curiosity stemming from the fear of missing out
- Stress tolerance: self-testing or grit, being curious about our own limits
- Social curiosity: creating deeper social connectedness by learning about others
- Thrill seeking: curiosity just for the thrill of it

Whatever your motivation, curiosity sets the stage for learning. Wanting to know more can be just as powerful as needing to find out for a specific purpose.

When treated with the respect they deserve, curiosity, wonder, and creativity connect and inspire each other in a never-ending, overlapping cycle. Shaming children for not knowing the "correct" answer will shut this process down.

Ali, a three-year-old, noticed there was no gold-colored crayon at preschool, so she asked her teachers if yellow and pink could make gold. Her teachers laughed, probably without thinking, but this child was still carrying the shame of that moment years later. In her mind, her teachers thought her idea was dumb. I [Laura] remember the moment in my own kindergarten experience when I couldn't remember how to make the numeral 6, so I carefully drew a domino six in the blank box next to six cartoon turtles. I was so upset that my teacher counted it wrong! Fifty years later, it still stings a little. Of course, we as teachers won't always say the right thing. As humans, we get busy and tired, but we can try to be aware of the seriousness of children's thinking and try to respond a little more appropriately as we gain experiences.

Constructivists, as well as the Next Generation Science Standards (NGSS Lead States, 2013), recommend inviting children to notice natural phenomena and then helping them to ask investigable questions. What makes a good question? It has to be open-ended. It can't be something the children already know. It can't be answered with a simple yes or no. It has to be something the children can investigate firsthand. Next, we provide materials for exploration that deepen children's understanding. By setting the stage for the unexpected, we help create events that challenge children's current thinking and spur them to learn more.

When we are curious about something, we are willing to engage and put forth the effort to learn more about it—we are naturally engaged. Curiosity is closely linked to a sense of wonder about the world around us. We found several definitions when we looked up *wonder* in various dictionaries:

- To admire
- To be amazed
- To be in awe
- To marvel
- Something strange or surprising
- A remarkable phenomenon

During workshops, Carla often brings in sweet gum balls after we look at the words and some quotes about wonder. Sweet gum balls are poky and have lots of holes, and often seeds come out. They are great spheres of wonder, sometimes compared to the coronavirus model commonly seen during the pandemic. Sweet gum trees have star-shaped leaves and can be found in various states of growth. So many things to wonder and be curious about. Given time to focus and explore, educators and children can come up with many observations and even more questions. Some listen for sounds or smell the sweet gum balls, while others feel the textures of the pointy parts. One educator wondered what was inside. She asked if it was okay to try to open it up. Following the "yes mentality" and knowing I had a whole basketful as well as a source where I could gather more, I said yes. She worked diligently at deconstructing the sweet gum ball. She found tools to help and continued working while we went on with the workshop. She eventually reached the core and was able to share her curiosity and what she learned with the rest of us. The bigger lesson may be persevering, having permission to explore, and following what we wonder about.

At a nature center during preschool time, one small group was exploring wind with a wind tunnel. They became enthusiastic as a feather or leaf floated up through the tube. One boy noticed the rock collection on display nearby and started getting curious about how a rock would react to the wind. Rather than telling him it wouldn't work, Carla let the child explore the idea on his own. Of course, this rock didn't move in the wind; however, a bigger lesson here was the freedom and ability to explore and experiment with the materials around him. His curiosity helped him drive his own learning and play.

This goes beyond curiosity to admiring, respecting, and getting to know the natural world in more depth. On a windy day, we grabbed a Loose Parts Nature Play kit on wind, which provided a tool (anemometer), books, and long, thin fabric strips from a garage sale for quick exploration on our site. We grabbed handfuls of leaves and threw them up in the air, watching them swirling around as they moved far from us. In experiencing wind, a natural phenomenon, with preschoolers we used all the senses—closing our eyes, smelling deeply of fall, feeling the wind on our skin, opening our mouths to taste the wind. Books such as *Noah Chases the Wind* by Michelle Worthington and *What Color Is the Wind?* by Anne Herbauts encouraged us to explore more deeply. We hid behind walls where the wind could not touch us. We noticed the wind moving the tall trees, pushing fallen leaves across the street, and flipping through flags. We felt the wind on our exposed faces and let our colorful fabrics go as children discovered the chain-link fence could catch them and hold them up in the wind, creating colorful art across the fence line.

Our wind experiences helped us explore with many senses. Rachel Carson (1956) urges us, "For most of us, knowledge of our world comes largely through sight, yet we look about with such unseeing eyes that we are partially blind. One way to open your eyes to unnoticed beauty is to ask yourself, 'What if I had never seen this before? What if I knew I would never see it again?'" Using all of our senses as we explore the world around us helps us to experience it in ways we might never explore otherwise.

"It is not half so important to know as to feel."

–Rachel Carson (1956)

Interaction with the wind provides creative opportunities to explore living loose parts for infants and toddlers as well. The simplest way is to invite children to notice the motion of grasses and trees in the wind. Hanging small mirrors on fishing line from the trees outside emphasizes the movement of even a gentle breeze, as do wind chimes and kinetic spinners. We can bring wind indoors by hanging scarves that flutter as we walk past. Young children love to experiment with things that fly with safely enclosed fans. Toddlers and preschoolers love to move things like feathers, flowers, and even unit blocks by blowing through a tube or straw at the spot where they touch the table.

Books to Inspire Curiosity in Us All

IN ADULTS

Bayles, David, and Ted Orlando. 2001. *Art and Fear: Observations on the Perils (and Rewards) of Artmaking*. Santa Cruz, CA: Image Continuum Press.

Behr, Gregg, and Ryan Rydzewski. 2021. *When You Wonder, You're Learning: Mr. Rogers' Enduring Lessons for Raising Creative, Curious, Caring Kids*. New York: Hachette.

Carson, Rachel. 2017. *The Sense of Wonder: A Celebration of Nature for Parents and Children.* New York: Harper Perennial.

Denmead, Ken. 2010. *Geek Dad: Awesomely Geeky Projects and Activities for Dads and Kids to Share.* New York: Avery.

Ruef, Kerry. 1992. *The Private Eye: Looking/Thinking by Analogy.* Seattle, WA: The Private Eye Project.

Smith, Keri. 2008. *How to Be an Explorer of the World: Portable Life Museum.* New York: Penguin.

Smith, Keri. 2012. *Wreck This Journal.* New York: Penguin.

IN CHILDREN

Archer, Micha. 2021. *Wonder Walkers.* New York: Nancy Paulsen Books.

Daywalt, Drew. 2013. *The Day the Crayons Quit.* New York: Philomel.

Ehlert, Lois. 2001. *Waiting for Wings.* New York: Harcourt.

Fox, Mem. 2006. *The Magic Hat.* New York: Clarion.

Gollub, Matthew. 2011. *The Jazz Fly.* Santa Rosa, CA: Tortuga Press.

Hall, Michael. 2011. *Perfect Square.* New York: Greenwillow Books.

Hutchins, Pat. 1987. *Changes, Changes.* New York: Aladdin.

Hutts Aston, Dianna. 2011. *Dream Something Big: The Story of the Watts Towers.* New York: Dial Books.

Jenkins, Steve. 2011. *Actual Size.* New York: Clarion.

Kerr, Judith. 2006. *The Tiger Who Came to Tea.* New York: HarperCollins.

Morris, Jackie. 2018. *The Barefoot Book of Classic Poems.* Concord, MA: Barefoot Books.

Portis, Antoinette. 2006. *Not A Box.* New York: HarperCollins.

Saltzberg, Barney. 2010. *Beautiful Oops!* New York: Workman Publishing.

Smith, Lane. 2017. *A Perfect Day.* New York: Roaring Brook Press.

Tryon, Leslie. 1994. *Albert's Alphabet.* New York: Aladdin.

Underwood, Deborah. 2020. *Outside In.* New York: Clarion.

OBSERVATIONAL HINDRANCES

As we consider embracing slowing down and noticing, we also may want to investigate ways our actions may take away from that natural curiosity in our classrooms.

While in a beautiful setting in Alaska at a wildlife refuge where we could see native mammals up close, Carla noticed one younger child, about three years old, engrossed in the rocks in the common area. The child was picking up the rocks, holding them, exchanging them for another, and observing the rocks closely. Her father tried to prompt her to go see the animals; however, the girl's focus remained on the rocks. She was curious and engaged with something seemingly simple—the fill gravel in the parking lot—while surrounded by animals she may never see again. Her father eventually scooped her up to go to the animal enclosures, leaving the precious rocks and that focused attention behind.

"Don't be afraid. Explore, touch, smell, feel, and be there in that moment. We don't have to understand all of it right now. If we keep asking questions, answers will come."

—Joe Rackley

We need to consider this as we tear children away from their curiosity to accommodate our schedules or a new activity rather than letting children be and explore at their own pace. It's a balancing act, but allowing choice and voice in how they explore can raise the curiosity-and-wonder factor. We awaken the wonder in our spaces as we embrace slowing down and noticing nature while we entertain our curiosity.

"Keep it simple. Projects, invitations, provocations, and so on, especially in early childhood education, can and should be repetitive, easy to replicate, 'risky' yet safe, schema based, and open-ended. Living loose parts tend to fit into these concepts with very little effort."

—Sara Evans

EMBRACING CURIOSITY

As we explore curiosity within the context of living loose parts, we can be the adult Rachel Carson (1956) was talking about when she said, "If a child is to keep alive his inborn sense of wonder . . . he needs the companionship of at least one adult who can share it, rediscovering with him the joy, excitement, and mystery of the world we live in." What characteristics do we educators need to cultivate so we can encourage and support this exploration of living loose parts? Modeling curiosity goes a long way! In the book *When You Wonder, You're Learning* (Behr and Rydzewski, 2021), the authors share a study around the typical "dancing raisin" experiment in which raisins are added to soda and the observer can see the raisin bobbing around in the bubbles. In a class where the teacher wondered aloud what might happen if they used Skittles candies instead of raisins, the children came up with more diverse ideas and options as variations on this exploration. It was as if permission to think outside the box had been given.

Family Engagement

Invite the families to participate in the children's curiosity and exploration. Family engagement might include special days or events, such as seasonal celebrations, hosting a sugar shack for making maple syrup, inviting a local naturalist in with an animal, or involving families in collecting loose parts for investigation.

Carla often sends home a paper bag in the fall with a note encouraging families to go on an autumn walk in their neighborhoods and to collect a few fallen treasures, with tips on responsible collecting. Each child is excited to share their experiences and what they have found. Carla brings in extra treasures in case a family forgets or is unable to do the activity.

Family members might have special skills or expertise to share with the group. Carla often stopped by her son's preschool after doing outdoor education with live animals at another preschool to share a snake, amphibians, or even a live turkey with the children and educators. A tree trimmer may have access to logs, branches, and tools to add more play options in the outdoor classroom. A gardener may share spent flowers and plant material to add to stone soup or aromatic concoctions.

Create classroom books about your living loose parts explorations that can be sent home for reading with the family. Allow families to create additional pages to add to the books, such as a winter exploration book, by sharing pictures, activities, and discoveries of how they interact with nature and the seasonal changes.

Consider inviting parents into the space as much as possible. Some schools use a cooperative model where each parent volunteers in some capacity, whether at the school or by completing tasks at home, such as making the weekly playdough. Spending time watching the children involved in risky play or digging for critters, along with seeing how the educators interact in these situations, often gives parents the confidence to facilitate these experiences on their own. Include parents in special staff development by having a shorter meeting directed at parents as the audience with practical, hands-on tips and inspiration. Share bite-sized quotes or data along with a picture of their child engaging in that practice. Pass along short articles. Form a book group to explore a concept in more depth.

Among the many ideas they share in the article "Celebrating Special Days with a Loose Parts Mindset," Gull, Levenson Goldstein, and Rosengarten (2023) suggest hosting a Family Nature Club. This can be arranged with early drop-off or pickup with time to linger and explore in our outdoor spaces together. "Find a free download to host a family nature club at Nature Explore. These activities are versatile, include loose parts, and can be incorporated as an aftercare nature club or a special celebration for the school. Download materials at natureexplore.org." On learninginplaces.org (n.d.), a set of tools to use with families is also available that can be used in any season, such as the Family Wondering Walk. Families record the weather and place while investigating a plant or animal in more depth with a sketch, details they notice, and what they wonder about the plant or animal. These notes can then be used as data in the classroom for additional explorations. Materials are available in Chinese, Spanish, and English.

Activating Curiosity through Sensory Play

In supporting sensory experiences, we may find that some students seek more or less sensory stimulation. On the *Tinkergarten* blog, Meghan Fitzgerald (2023) suggests the following to support sensory development in children.

* Being in nature can be the ultimate sensory experience. Being outdoors also allows children to seek their own level of sensory stimulation.
* Recognize different sensory desires in children. Some have more need for full immersion in mud, smearing it all over their bodies, while others may only be interested in interacting with mud through a tool such as a stick. Warming up our senses before using them more fully can help children turn on this exploration tool. For example, we might rub our hands together while singing before we enter mud play.
* Broaden the play options and provide tools for inclusivity. While a child may not initially want to touch mud with their hands or feet, using a stick, leaf, or magnifying glass may give a choice for how the child interacts with the mud. Overwhelmed children may need some support by lessening the sensory stimulation or changing environments.
* Engage in our own sensory play! Exploring our own sensory investigations can do wonders as we model curiosity and engage with the world around us.

"The senses, being explorers of the world, open the way to knowledge."

–Maria Montessori

Each month, Carla has been visiting one school with an open-ended investigation for the children and then professional development for the educators. Often, they just slow down and explore. Beyond the art teacher, many educators had not interacted much with natural clay. In setting up a clay provocation, it was interesting to see the comfort level of each person with the medium. Some oozed and smeared clay exuberantly. Others only interacted with tools initially but then later explored the clay and water with their hands. One abstained from touching the clay but interacted with the people, concepts, and ideas. Some integrated nature as part of their clay experience by finding natural loose parts to create a face on a tree or a hedgehog. By simply exploring the possibilities of clay, each could find a good sensory balance.

Slowing down lets children and adults take time to explore the concept of sit spots, add plants to their spaces, and create prompts or investigations to observe nature. Our programs may not include all of these elements, but we can play around to find the right mix for the needs of the children, our spaces, and our educational philosophies. No matter the setting, we can find and enhance nature around us, getting to know the natural rhythms as we slow down and observe life happening. We also can build respect for and honor nature while we get curious about all these living creatures and organisms.

CHAPTER 3

Honoring All Living Things

"First of all, I believe nature is necessary for our survival. Secondly, it is our responsibility to take care of the world where we live. Lastly, we must have respect and understand the importance of ecosystems. As a small child, I gained a love for nature by observing my family's love for the outdoors."

–Angela Holms-Krober

We want to tread lightly upon the Earth, honoring the living natural world by respecting plants and creatures. We want to put things back where we found them. As the park sign says, "Take only memories. Leave only footprints." Observe with respect, interact with grace and courtesy, and model kindness. Children, by themselves, can't clean up the world's oceans or save the rainforests, but they can pick up trash on the playground and sort the classroom recyclables. We can teach conservation and ecology in local, doable bits that aren't overwhelming to children or their families and, in doing so, set the stage for a lifetime of stewardship.

In the contributions on the topic of living loose parts, we found strong themes of honoring nature and reciprocity. Several contributors share how honoring nature shapes us. While each program is unique, the responsibility for and honor of caring for the Earth emerges through interactions with living loose parts.

Help children feel confident in engaging with loose parts by starting with things found nearby. With toddlers, just collecting pinecones or rocks on a walk is an exciting activity. We also talk about reciprocity and, as Robin Wall Kimmerer, author of *Braiding Sweetgrass*, says, the "honorable harvest." We don't take all; we take only what we need. We give thanks for the

> materials that nature has shared with us. Thanking a tree for the beautiful leaves or thanking a plant for a fruit can help instill in children the idea of our reliance on a healthy environment for our own health and sustenance, as well as build empathy for other beings.
>
> —Sheila Williams Ridge

How does caring for the Earth become part of your explorations? We can all consider ourselves part of nature and help children develop concepts such as honor, respect, care, and reciprocity as we interact with the world around us.

Considering Indigenous Perspectives

One way to connect with reciprocity and honor nature is by considering the perspectives and voices of Indigenous peoples. While not every person in a culture shares the same ideas and beliefs, it is important to find and honor authentic voices that have been silenced for too long. Online library searches and Google Scholar are making it much easier to locate native authors and illustrators. Also, do a bit of research to confirm whether popular myths, legends, and stories about Native people are based in fact. Do you know about the Indigenous people who are living, or once lived, on the land where you are today? How can you find out more about them? How might you incorporate the perspectives, language, and knowledge of these cultures into your practice?

Carla has been getting to know the local Indigenous communities where she lives in northern Indiana: the Pokagon Band of Potawatomi and the Miami Tribe of Oklahoma. She follows both groups on social media, has learned a few key phrases, attends powwows and other gatherings that are open to the public, and listens as local tribal members speak about their history and how they continue to live today. For example, she has worked with the local tribal Head Start program and watched cultural practices as an offering was made before children played with the mud. In a statewide webinar, Carla worked with Erin Burggraf from the Pokagon Band of Potawatomi to amplify Native voices around the importance of Indigenous perspectives in children's literature. Together, they created a book list for the *International Journal for Early Childhood Environmental Educators*. The suggested books are all by Native authors and share authentic points of view.

"Humans have always been connected to the land. We have a deep and inescapable relationship with our natural world, for without it, there is no life for us. It's time to rekindle that love affair and become guardians of what we hold so dear."

—Megan Gessler

Books with Indigenous Perspectives

Arita, Vera. 2014. *Alphabet Hukilau in Hawaii.* Kāne'Ohe, HI: BeachHouse Publishing.

Flett, Julie. 2021. *We All Play.* Vancouver, BC: Greystone Books.

Goade, Michaela. 2022. *Berry Song.* New York: Little, Brown Books for Young Readers.

Greendeer, Danielle, Anthony Perry, and Alexis Bunten. 2022. *Keepunumuk: Weeâchumun's Thanksgiving Story.* Watertown, MA: Charlesbridge.

Lindstrom, Carole. 2020. *We Are Water Protectors.* New York: Roaring Brook Press.

Lonzano, Christin. 2015. *Island Toes.* Honolulu, HI: Bess Press.

Louie, Ren. 2022. *Drum from the Heart.* Victoria, BC: Medicine Wheel Publishing.

Marshall, Albert, and Louise Zimanyi. 2023. *Walking Together.* Toronto, ON: Annick Press.

Robertson, Joanne. 2020. *Nibi Is Water.* Toronto, ON: Second Story Press.

Sorell, Traci. 2018. *We Are Grateful: Otsaliheliga.* Watertown, MA: Charlesbridge

Carla also leads a graduate course on intercultural environmental education in which she brings students to a new place to learn about the flora, fauna, and culture and to practice building their environmental education skills. During the course, she suggests that the students practice cultural humility and defer to the local voices, being curious rather than holding tight to what the students know, and being willing to change their minds and assumptions. Spending time with people from a local culture is essential, as is building relationships with individuals rather than lumping all people into one group. Her course has included a three-week trip to Hawaii. To prepare, they started learning some Native Hawaiian language using an app, as well as key words connected to the topic of study, such as our *kuleana* (privilege/honor of being responsible) to protect the *'aina* (land). They understood how these concepts were important to the local culture. In visits to schools, they noticed posters on the walls emphasizing these concepts and were able to connect the concepts they shared with the Hawaiian cultural principles of *mālama* (to take care of, preserve, protect) and *pono* (doing the right thing). They found children's books written by local Hawaiians illustrating the stories and concepts, to share with groups and to use as part of their own study. Students participated in locally available cultural activities, learning how to twist basic leis and natural-fiber hats. They observed at a local forest school, seeing how language and local natural loose parts were part of the play and learning. They also offered their own loose parts invitations for the children to explore.

"Without a connection to nature, we grow a population that is detached and can watch entire ecosystems vanish without a thought or concern. Nature is full of textures, sensations, colors, patterns, life in even the most extreme environments. Without it, we don't exist."

–Joe Rackley

Environmental Kinship

Rather than being separate from nature, many people are recognizing that, as humans, we are in relationship with nature. Environmental Kinship International advocates for four areas of connection: learning about, in, with, and for nature in developmentally appropriate ways.

- Learning about nature: the study of the natural world
- Learning in nature: affordances provided in nature
- Learning with nature: forming kinship with the natural world
- Learning for nature: recognizing the role of reciprocity in humans' connections with the rest of nature

They explain *kinship* as, "rooted in a deep kind of knowing that includes, but goes beyond, cognitive understanding. Humans, like other living things, are social beings. We live in relationship to others, not just with other humans, but with the entire natural world. Our evolutionary roots are in nature. This rootedness is an essential part of our physical reality, but it's also part of our emotional, psychological, and spiritual reality. We are ecological beings. Kinship recognizes this reality as being significant for all human beings" (Fox et al., 2022).

Environmental kinship can be a guiding framework for considering ourselves part of nature and for our interactions with living loose parts. This kinship urges us to study, spend ample time in nature, create relationships with our special places and natural encounters, and be reciprocal in our relationship with the natural world.

As we develop a reciprocal relationship with nature and see ourselves as nature, we can model care and respect for the natural world around us for children and families. We explore additional practical tips for including living loose parts in our settings in chapter 4.

CHAPTER 4

Practical Tips for Incorporating Living Loose Parts

We've explored the what and why of living loose parts, as well as the importance of slowing down to connect to nature and of honoring all living things. Next, let's consider how to engage with living loose parts. By getting outside in all seasons, setting up spaces for outdoor exploration, enhancing habitats, and making space for critters, we can encounter many living loose parts in our spaces.

Plan for the Elements and Human Needs

To embrace getting outside in all seasons, we may need to plan for the elements. Each program should have general weather guidelines pertinent to their area to help them make decisions. In some areas, educators may need a plan for extreme heat or humidity. Others may need to watch the wind, air quality, tides, or windchill factor. Having general guidelines compliant with local regulations allows as much safe time outside as possible. You may need to plan for adding shade sails, providing drinking water, or inspecting trees for dead limbs that might fall in the wind. Be sure to have a first-aid kit available at all times, as well as emergency plans and shelter when needed for more extreme weather.

You will likely need gear to keep everyone comfortable outside. Depending on your climate, that may mean raincoats, rain hats, and galoshes; parkas, gloves, and snow boots; or sunhats and water bottles. The Fenner Nature Center in Lansing, Michigan, has a lending library of materials available for checkout. In particular, they host a whole classroom set of rainsuits that can be used for two weeks at a time. Educators can try the clothing out before they buy suits for their space. Many programs have a lending closet that they fill by scouring thrift stores and garage sales for gear and by asking for any outgrown weather gear to pass on to future families. Consider approaching similar programs in your area or writing grants to get the funding for equipment. Programs have also received discounts when contacting a company directly and making a bulk purchase. Sometimes, the fee for weather gear is rolled into the class fees, with options for financial supplementation or scholarships. Don't forget to provide gear for the adults in your program, too.

Store the gear in an organized fashion to make accessing it easier. Share tips with your local educator organizations about what is working for your weather elements, and check with local organizations for others in your area about how their gear is working for them. For example, Northern Illinois Nature Preschool Association, Minnesota Early Childhood Outdoors, Texas Children in Nature Network, Nature Niños New Mexico, and Early Childhood Hoosiers Outdoors all host regional events and forums where educators can ask questions and share how the logistics work in their spaces. There is power in connecting with other professionals in our area to overcome these local challenges.

When we plan for the elements, we can get out in most types of weather with the children. A child with appropriate gear and precautions can get comfortably curious about puddle play, exploring ice, or experimenting with heat on beeswax.

> Being in a place that experiences long winters, the biggest factor to my connection with nature has probably been embracing outdoor activity year-round. Visiting local Indigenous centers for insight and acknowledging their ties to this land has contributed greatly to this stance.
>
> —Sara Evans

> Winter is a huge barrier for educators and families. It's important to help others understand how living loose parts can work in the middle of winter with frigid temperatures. I am leading my "Wonders of Winter" program now with thirty educators to help them see how they can create rich learning in winter.
>
> —April Zajko

LOGISTICS OF TOILETING AND WASHING HANDS OUTSIDE

Two main issues that potentially get in the way of a licensed program spending more time outside are washing hands and toileting concerns. To comply with licensing and to allow outdoor time, many groups have gotten creative.

For handwashing, be sure to use eco-friendly soap that will be safe for the plants, such as a castile soap. If you lack access to running water outside, try providing warm water dispensed with a water jug, a portable sprayer with a hose and nozzle, or a spray or squirt bottle.

Many programs are dedicating space to outdoor diapering or toilet options. Others use a potty chair or install a compostable toilet. One program Carla works with uses a pop-up tent and a small camping toilet. Each day, the program brings the materials out to the area where they spend the majority of their time.

Prepare for Learning

Living loose parts can be as simple as ourselves as humans and how we interact with the variables or other humans in our environment. Heather Taylor of the Outside School in California recognizes the power of the human brain as a loose part. She shares, "I purposefully don't bring in many additional materials, so we have to make do with what's before us. We also do volunteer work, so there will be tools for digging, planting, and picking up litter. Others using the park or working there also can be 'loose parts' who are a big part of what we do."

For her work with elementary students, Taylor recommends bringing a backpack that contains the following:

- Mechanical pencils, grid paper, and dry-erase markers
- A dissecting kit and magnifying glass
- Knives, scissors, and a multitool
- A metal ruler (imperial and metric) and variety of dice
- Plastic and soapstone animals
- Rope

Consider the essentials you would need for your setting, needs, and the interests of the children you work with. Some programs provide each child with a drawstring backpack with a few basics, such as a journal, colored pencils, and a magnifying glass. Include investigation tools in your space, both inside and out, such as magnifying glasses, binoculars, clipboards and paper, bug jars, scooping nets, tweezers, buckets, shovels, and viewing habitats. You can also consider creating kits and preparing for collections.

LIVING LOOSE PARTS COLLECTIONS AND KITS

As the children become more immersed in the natural world, they will want to collect some of the things they discover. All preschool-aged children are collectors. If you don't believe it, ask them to check their pockets. They will be just as surprised as you to find what's inside. Things just seem to fall in there: rocks, acorns, sticks, small cars, and wilting dandelions. We can build on their natural impulses to collect and organize objects into groups. The respect and honor mentioned previously will be essential as children build their own collections and use the natural resources in their environments for play. A simple container like an egg carton can hold these collected treasures while they are being examined.

Children's Books That Feature Collections

Grice, Gordon. 2015. *Cabinet of Curiosities: Collecting and Understanding the Wonders of the Natural World*. New York: Workman Publishing Group.

Feagan, Alice. 2021. *The Collectors*. Toronto, ON: Kids Can Press.

Marzollo, Jean, and Walter Wick. *I Spy* series. New York: Scholastic.

Montgomery, Heather. 2024. *What's in Your Pocket? Collecting Nature's Treasures*. Watertown, MA: Charlesbridge.

Radcliffe, Austin. 2016. *Things Organized Neatly: The Art of Arranging the Everyday*. New York: Rizzoli International.

Sanchez, Michael. 2017. *Natural History Collector: Hunt, Discover, Learn!* Beverly, MA: Quarry Books.

Spires, Ashley. 2013. *The Most Magnificent Thing*. Toronto, ON: Kids Can Press.

Steiner, Joan. *Look-Alikes* series. New York: Little, Brown Books for Young Readers.

You can also build kits for responsive explorations around any emerging topic. Carla calls her exploration kits Loose Parts Nature Play kits or Loose Parts Starts. No matter the name, these kits are a start for—but never an end to—play. The items, combined with the participants and setting, allow for rich interaction.

Kits allow teachers to grab and go when they notice children being curious about something. Kits are versatile, help you find your stuff quickly, and make materials available and accessible for more people. The kits can also help you be flexible about how you are using supplies and loose parts. These dynamic options, often curated by the children, are intended to be used for embracing our natural settings, such as the outdoor classroom garden or neighborhood park. Kits can be used in a variety of settings. Grab one for storytime, to take on a hike, as we follow children's interests, as an option on family days, as part of children's free choice time, or to rotate. Allow children to choose what kits to take outside each day. You can also let families check them out from your center and take them for use at home.

Often, kits can be made with what you already have. But, if you know that you would like to gather more materials to put together focused kits, you can collect things from nature and garage sales. If you need more money to create kits, you might also seek specific grants, ask for donations, or hold a special fundraiser. As you gather materials, keep an inventory so you know what you have and what will need. Group like items together so you can easily understand how many and what type of each material you have.

Consider a theme or type of kit, what materials might be needed around an emerging topic, such as books, dramatic play props, additional loose parts, a container or bag for materials, labels, and any additional notes, suggestions, or ideas to go with the kit, such as a cool space to use the kit.

* **Book extensions:** Children's books make great kit topics. Consider, for example, *Not a Stick* by Antoinette Portis, *Mama Built a Little Nest* by Jennifer Ward, *Woodpecker Wham!* by April Pulley Sayre, or *An Egg Is Quiet* and *A Nest Is Noisy* by Dianna Hutts Aston.
* **Animal focus:** Choose any animal that lives in your area: mammals, birds, fish, insects, reptiles, amphibians, arthropods, and more.

- **Building:** Include open-ended materials such as wooden blocks, mini bricks, and cardboard tools.
- **Play:** Provide materials for a mud kitchen, music and movement, water play, dramatic play, or fort play.
- **Art:** Provide open-ended materials such as playdough, watercolors or paint, paintbrushes or paper, small loose parts, and chalk.
- **General outdoor tools:** Include tweezers, magnifying glasses, binoculars, twine, buckets, paper, clipboards, writing utensils, and so on.

Kit containers can be clear plastic bags, such as those used in libraries, muslin drawstring backpacks, zippable backpacks, reusable grocery totes, large IKEA bags, crates, baskets, dishpans, or even a wagon. Be sure to label the kits. To do this, you might use stencils, laminated tags and pictures, fabric labels, a numbered system, child-created decorations, or wooden laser-engraved labels. Include a list of what belongs in the kit, so anyone using or borrowing it can make sure everything gets put back.

Finding storage to make kits accessible is essential. Consider hooks on a wall at child height, a cart of kits, big storage bags made by adding elastic or drawstrings to the tops of old pillowcases, a rod with S hooks, large tubs, cubbies, or an outdoor shed where you can find what is needed quickly and easily. Regularly purge and evaluate bags and materials. Check for anything that has become chipped, splintered, or broken, and assess the risk.

Think about what living loose parts kits might work in your situation. How might you try one out with the children? For example, a kit focused on beavers might have the following materials:

- Beaver pelt and skull
- Pictures of beaver lodges and dams
- *I'm Done!* by Gretchen Brandenburg McLellan
- *The Lodge That Beaver Built* by Randi Sonenshine
- Dramatic play props: Cardboard beaver tails with twine
- Additional loose parts: Sticks, bucket and shovel for mud, hollow wooden blocks, such as Guidecraft mini hollow blocks

Carla put this kit together for her program. For funding, most items were repurposed materials they had in storage, with tails made with cardboard. She put the materials in a muslin drawstring bag and added a tie-on label. As an additional reminder of some possibilities for using the kit without limiting the applications, she included a note: "Use this in the block area or the large loose parts area outside, and/or provide additional building options, such as large loose parts kits (Nudelkart, Rigamajig), straw building sets, boxes, clean empty cans, etc."

Set Up Spaces for Living Loose Parts

Outdoor classrooms can be a perfect backdrop for encountering living loose parts. Nicholson (1971) suggests that our spaces should be laboratory-like with opportunities to explore, invent, and have fun. He also suggests blurring the inside and outside. Ideally, it's great to have open access between the inside and outside spaces with an educator in each space. Play, fun, and learning can happen inside as well as outside, as children do not clearly differentiate between the two when it's based on their ideas and they are the primary participants in setting up and using the learning environments.

> **"In one of the college courses that I teach, 'Growing Outdoor Classrooms,' I encourage educators to have a raised bed with living materials for children to play with. Trimming chives, mint, or lemon balm (all plants that grow back quickly) is an amazing way to add a sensory element to children's play!"**
>
> –April Zajko

You can enhance both your indoor and outdoor spaces in many ways. Add herbs for cutting, flowers that provide color, and interesting gourds. Additionally, bring cuttings and fresh plants from your home gardens and other spaces. Ask on social media for options for flowers and get to know local people with a green thumb who may have garden clippings that would work in your space. A program in Michigan has a large church-supported garden nearby. The compost pile is often filled with corn stalks, spent flowers, and other delights that would make a perfect addition to mud soup or used seasonally for building. In more natural settings, Carla also helps children learn which plants, such as the native trillium, may need protection and which are rather invasive, such as vinca, and can be used in play.

- **Fragrance gardens:** When planting garden boxes and flower beds at your school, consider the scents. Teach children to gently rub the leaves or cup their hands around the plant to release the scent without damaging the plant. Good options include herbs such as basil, thyme, lemon balm, and rosemary, as well as local flowers. Perhaps include lavender, crepe myrtle, pansies, and roses.

- **Sensory gardens:** Include scents and consider texture, such as lamb's ear, succulents, and broccoli; sound, such as grasses and nandina that rustle in the wind; sight, such as variations in shades of green or a variety of flowers; and taste, such as edible herbs and flowers such as mint, basil, pansies, nasturtium, lavender, and honeysuckle.

- **Nature artifact tables:** Consider a touch-and-feel table with antlers, skull replicas, turtle shells, bones, snakeskin, discarded insect shells, animals in resin, feathers from a farm or store, furs, owl pellets, shells, seeds, nuts or galls with animal exit holes, evidence of animals such as wood with beaver or woodpecker chiseling activity, a track casting, and so on. Carla finds these in a variety of places on walks and by letting people know what she is looking for. Be sure to check your local regulations, especially for turtle shells, feathers, and nest collecting.

- **Play videos or sounds of nature:** Play recordings of bird calls, rain, waterfalls, wind, and so on, as well as bird- and nest-cam streaming inside the classroom. You can find wildlife webcams on the US Fish and Wildlife Service website (https://www.fws.gov/story/wildlife-webcams) and on the National Park Service website (https://www.nps.gov/subjects/watchingwildlife/webcams.htm).

Trees offer so many benefits and opportunities, along with adding plenty of loose parts, such as sticks, pinecones, acorns, and other natural treasures. If you don't have a tree, consider planting some.

> I encourage people to start small by being intentional in the natural loose parts that they bring into their space. Creating a vision map of the outdoor classroom they want to develop, and sharing that vision with their community, can make their learning space come alive with plants and materials that they offer.
>
> —April Zajko

Exploring Loose Parts with Live Animals

Why should we intentionally connect children with animals? Children are naturally curious and enthusiastic about animals. Involving live animals brings excitement and a buzz of interest. Interactions with animals provide opportunities to practice empathy. Children have a natural affinity for other living things. Animals provide opportunities to learn to care. Children begin to notice the needs of animals and help care for them through interaction and building responsibilities around food, shelter, and water for the animals.

Through play, children may take on the persona of the animal and consider how the animal may or may not enjoy a particular activity. Seeing an animal move helps children reflect on their own body's motion and wonder about how another organism survives.

Pets are often part of families. Children interact with dogs, cats, hamsters, and guinea pigs. Pets become friends to the children. The care, concern, and connection children naturally have for nature often transfer over into other relationships.

Animals are part of the living markers of our spaces. They help children develop a sense of place. Getting to know the local fauna helps connect children to where they live. Direct experiences with animals build knowledge of and experience with living things. Rather than just reading about animals, direct observation and experience offer children a different way of knowing and learning. Animals offer cognitive challenges. What do they need? How can we capture their interest?

Animals offer sensory input—visual, tactile, smell, sound, and proprioception—when children help care for the animal through the heavy work of carrying food, water, or cages. Children can see similarities and differences and practice the science skill of observation, the literacy skill of recording, and the math skill of comparison. Animals can help people process feelings. Children often feel calmer when therapy animals are nearby, giving them room to process trauma and strong emotions.

Animals have special abilities, such as a husky's ability to run and pull things, a dog's ability to smell things that humans cannot, a gecko's ability to climb vertical walls and hang onto ceilings, a flea's ability to jump two hundred times its own body length, a squirrel's ability to cache its food, a bat's ability to echolocate its prey, or a beaver's ability to engineer the environment by building dams. As children learn about animal superpowers, they can also reflect on their own special abilities.

Bringing nature into our classrooms can make a powerful impact. Including live plants and animals really adds interest to the learning environment. There are many ways we can make this happen, whether you prefer starting with baby steps or jumping in with both feet:

- **Observe in the natural habitat:** Take children to a local park or beach, or simply head outside. Carla worked in one program situated at a nature center on ten acres in a city surrounded by industry. Hiking the trails with the children, they might find a barred owl, birds, chipmunks, a snake, toads, lots of squirrels, and fish and frogs in a small pond. In other settings with the children, she often watched squirrels outside the windows as they leaped from tree to tree. Turning over a log or board often reveals many insects and other critters. Be sure to put the log back after observing. At your own school, add a trail cam to see what might be visiting at night or on weekends.

- **Add a classroom pet:** What a wonderful way to learn empathy and interact with living loose parts on a regular basis! Before undertaking care for a classroom pet, be sure to thoroughly investigate the animal's needs, necessary care and supplies, and habits. Some classrooms have gotten hermit crabs only to find they are nocturnal and take more care than expected.

  Kathleen McGee Wieske cautions, "I would always investigate the animal's needs and adaptability to being around children before investing in them . . . I am a firm believer that classroom pets benefit children immensely and are a valuable learning experience, when you have the right match."

  Snails, Madagascar hissing cockroaches, worms, and betta fish can be easy beginning classroom pets; although, others report having guinea pigs, hamsters, rabbits, chickens, silkworms, rats, axolotls, stick insects, aquatic frogs, hermit crabs, and dogs. One even had a pig! To help with maintenance, some programs contract out the aquarium or barnyard cleaning to a local expert.

- **Raise young animals:** Consider hatching chickens or quail in an incubator or raising caterpillars to the butterfly stage. This is not a long commitment and will give children opportunities to observe regular changes in the life cycle. It's so mesmerizing! Have a plan for releasing the caterpillar or rehoming the birds. Some areas have programs to put incubators in schools and then arrange for the chicks to go to a local farm. Ideally, we like to find native caterpillars in our local area, but you can also buy them online.

  At the Early Learning Center in northern Indiana, the Nature Explore–certified outdoor classroom had a monarch waystation with native plants. The children noticed caterpillars and worked with (human) adults to create a simple enclosure to meet the caterpillars' needs. Each day, they fed them fresh milkweed, gave them fresh water, and cleaned the enclosure. Later, the children had the magical experience of releasing the butterflies.

- **Form animal partnerships:** The Lilly Center for Lakes and Streams (https://lakes.grace.edu) in northern Indiana provides aquariums with fish from the local waterways. Staff from the program even set up the aquariums and came in to clean them. The Piedmont Wildlife Center in North Carolina will bring animal ambassadors to local classrooms. Learn more on their website (https://www.piedmontwildlifecenter.org/atschool-programs). Find out what programs may be available in your area.

- **Offer pet sitting:** A local science center needed pet sitters while it went through a move. Carla took care of the Madagascar hissing cockroaches, turtles, and a snake that could then be used short-term in classrooms.

- **Collect (and return) wildlife:** Carla gathers insects, crayfish, tadpoles, frogs, and turtles on her property to bring into the classroom for the day, then releases them later that evening. Note that a fishing license is often required to collect aquatic animals. Check and follow local regulations where you live. Be sure to return the animals to the wild promptly.

- **Invite therapy animals:** Many programs offer opportunities to read with a dog or have special time with a therapy animal. The American Kennel Club offers a list of therapy dog programs (https://www.akc.org/sports/title-recognition-program/therapy-dog-program/therapy-dog-organizations/). Look online for local read-to-a-dog (or cat or bunny) programs in your area.

- **Apply for grant funding:** If money is a concern, consider applying for funding through a Pets in the Classroom grant. You can learn more at their website (https://petsintheclassroom.org).

Anytime we consider introducing a live animal to the learning space, we need to make sure we have planned for the safety of both the animal and the children. We must teach respectful interactions by modeling the behaviors we expect and monitoring the children closely. For example, Charlotte Wood-Wilson's program enacted a no-kill policy. When a child saw a spider on the playground and prepared to stomp it, Charlotte reminded him of the book they'd been reading, *Charlotte's Web*. The children immediately said, "Oh, yeah! It is Charlotte!" The child who had been prepared to stomp it suddenly became the spider's self-appointed guardian, telling everyone on the playground to be careful as they passed.

"Consider the animals' needs. It is better not to have live animals if you can't care for them. Some turtles may outlive you. Once, I was able to borrow pets—a bird, a lizard, a frog—for a few days at a time from a local pet shop."

–Charlotte Wood-Wilson

Check your local regulations and conduct a benefit-risk analysis with an administrator or coteacher. A benefit-risk analysis lists the benefits of a particular activity, potential issues that might arise, and ways to help keep the situation safe. The analysis will help you decide whether the benefits outweigh any potential issues. Be aware of known allergies and signs of allergic reactions. Have a response plan in place, with clear instructions for substitute teachers and new staff, before introducing live animals to children.

There are lots of ways to give children opportunities to interact with and observe animals. The following is a list of suggestions; your location will determine which animals are part of your ecosystem.

- **Classroom pets to consider (may be short-term):**
  - Gerbil, hamster, or guinea pig
  - Hermit crab
  - Mealworms
  - Spider
  - Goldfish or guppies
  - Rabbit
  - Hissing cockroaches
  - Caterpillars to butterflies
  - Eggs to chicks
- **Classroom visitors:**
  - Zoo ambassador animals
  - Aquarium "water on wheels" programs
  - Family pets for special events
  - Therapy animals
  - Animal rehabilitation organizations
- **Outdoor animals to look for:**
  - Ladybugs
  - Crickets
  - Grasshoppers
  - Butterflies
  - Beetles
  - Roly-poly bugs (also called pill bugs)
  - Earthworms
- **Opportunities to observe animals on the playground or school property:**
  - Handheld or window-mounted hummingbird feeder
  - Classroom window nest box
  - Nesting balls
  - Squirrel or bird feeder
  - Bug or bee hotel
  - Frog, butterfly, or bat house
  - Birdbath, butterfly puddler, or saucer of water
  - Trail camera
- **Animals to observe at a nearby park:**
  - Squirrels
  - Birds
  - Fish
  - Chipmunks
  - Deer
  - Caterpillars
  - Weevils in acorns
- **Animals to observe in a nearby stream:**
  - Minnows
  - Sunfish or perch
  - Crayfish
  - Frogs
  - Toads
  - Turtles
  - Dragonflies
  - Macroinvertebrates

While taking a graduate research course, I [Laura] scheduled an observation in a friend's science classroom. He directed me to sit in the back of the room. While taking notes, I kept noticing a soft "crunch, crunch, crunch" sound, but I couldn't be sure where it was coming from. When I finally turned for a closer look at the 50-gallon aquarium at my back, I could see it was filled with hundreds, maybe thousands, of roly-polies. They were transforming a layer of dry oak leaves into compost. You could see the line of fresh soil rising on the glass as the leaves were "processed" by these tiny terrestrial crustaceans.

What resources are in your area to have animal visitors at your site? Carla asked in the Loose Parts Play group on social media about how they include animals in their spaces.

> Gemma Nicholl Medina has a variety of animals: "Silkie chickens, bantam chickens, rats, fish, rabbits, ducks, turtles, tortoises, Jackson chameleons . . . I live in Hawai'i so that is about the limit. Guinea pigs are the best! I would not have a classroom without pets. They add so much opportunity for connection, caring, science . . . I could go on!"
>
> Lana Mccaulley mentioned, "Pets teach us about nutrition, habitats, empathy, how to take care of things smaller than us, and ultimately and sadly, death."
>
> Debi Desmond-Jones has a dog that visits Monday, Wednesday, and Friday. She says the dog "visits classes and 'listens' to the younger children reading, which they absolutely LOVE!"
>
> Michael Fritzen asserted, "Live animals teach kids compassion, respect for animals, how to care for a living thing, may spark a love for animals, and provide opportunities for kids who can't have animals at home. Also, imagine all that you do with a live animal, story writing, science, art, language arts, and more. Consider something easy like a guinea pig, a mouse, rat, insects, snails, or salamander. All are easy to care for and low cost."
>
> Cherry Mays shared, "Fifteen years ago, a child's discovery on the playground led me to bring living things into the classroom. We discovered that the strange insects on the trees were ladybug larvae. This became a several-week study that I re-created for many years with the help of instructional insect suppliers. My confidence in working with living loose parts led me to write a grant for a class pet, and I have kept a fish tank in my room for the last ten years. Children are drawn to the fish. I discovered that even non-English speaking and nonverbal children will react and communicate on some level while interacting with living loose parts. Over the years, we have explored caterpillars and documented their life cycle. We carefully held, measured, and compared earthworms. We waited patiently for snails and hermit crabs to crawl out of their shells, predicting, describing, and recording how long they took to emerge. We planned and constructed habitats for roly-polies and read that they could breathe with gills

> in the soil. We planted seeds and observed that each seed had parts above and below the soil that supported how it developed and [observed] how our actions affect them. We cared for, harvested, and ate vegetables we had never tried in the cafeteria before and looked forward to [them] after the experience. We were amazed to see how quickly the tadpoles changed and had to rearrange our graph on the interactive whiteboard to match how many were in each stage of development. Then, we all shared their release into my garden through Zoom when we were learning from home in May 2020."

Around Thanksgiving, Carla has asked on social media for a lead on borrowing a turkey to bring to the preschool for an outdoor visit. Another preschool in Indiana with a Nature Explore–certified outdoor classroom has an outside enclosure. They borrow a turkey from a local farmer for a couple of weeks each November to get to know the animal over a longer period of time. It goes back to the farm when the visit is over. Some farmers may be willing to bring animals in for a petting zoo for the day as well.

Local wildlife rehabilitation services are often interested in doing educational programs. Dennis Badke, a local [Indiana] rehabber, has brought an owl, fox, skunk (de-scented), and weasel into local early childhood settings for Carla. Local parks, city biologists, botanical gardens, zoos, and nature centers may have live animal encounters they can bring to classrooms as well. You may choose to let professionals take care of the real experiences.

You can buy live fishing bait to allow children (with clean, moist hands) to explore and get to know worms. Have a plan for disposal (or go fishing with them!) after the visit. The book *This Is a Book to Read with a Worm* by Jodi Wheeler-Toppen can be shared during worm experiences, as it guides the reader through simple exercises, such as finding the worm's face, investigating its reaction to light and rubbing alcohol, and visualizing the digestive system.

Go on a field trip to places with animals. Check out local nature centers, city and county parks, pet stores, zoos, aquariums, farms, petting zoos, natural habitats of the animals, or a walking tour to expand your opportunities to interact with animals in nature. Watch for natural habitats of the animals, such as a ditch on the side of the road in spring for tadpoles, the roost tree for turkey vultures each night, or the gathering spot for sandhill cranes in the fall. Consider mapping your resources and options.

Enhancing Habitats

As you consider living loose parts in our classrooms (including our outdoor classrooms), consider what animals need. All animals need food, shelter, water, and a place to raise their young. Consider where you live and what can be sustained in your area, as well as the outdoor spaces you frequent. How might you enhance the likelihood of living loose parts sharing our outdoor spaces?

First, find nature in your space. One of Carla's favorite things is to go into school settings and help them find nearby nature that is being overlooked due to busy schedules and regular routines. Check the view out the windows. How can these become portals of nature where children can get a small glimpse of the living loose parts outside? Perhaps place a bird feeder or watering station outside the window, or create a garden of plants that attract insects and butterflies. Go along the fence and see if there are hidden gems of green matter that might host natural elements. Explore outside the fence, too. What other areas could the children explore on a walking field trip? Some schools have a blanket permission slip signed at the beginning of the year that allows educators to take the children outside the fence at school and in nearby community spaces. At times, extra adults are needed, especially if you will be near water.

At one school Carla visits, she uses the whole outdoor space with the children and educators to help them get to know the nearby trees, the community garden area, shrubs, and other aspects. While the fenced area with grass, climbing structures, swings, and sand is more traditional, the area outside the fence offers more variety in nature. When the children explore squirrels, they can find a nearby oak tree with acorns on the ground and sometimes even find evidence of squirrels having eaten the nuts. With one living loose parts exploration, they spent time around an evergreen outside the building. The children could play with puppets and stuffed animals in and around the tree and nearby bushes as the children enveloped themselves in the boughs. One of the teachers got teary-eyed as it reminded her of her childhood play in the bushes and what a magical time it was. She had worked at the preschool for thirteen years and had never noticed the tree was even there. Now it is one of their favorite spaces for nature play!

Get to know your space and options better by using a map tool such as Google Maps to note nearby green spaces. One school has a walking path nearby that they use regularly. Create a map of your space as well, noting loose parts options over the seasons. Get curious about what is in your space. Watch for evidence of animals in your space, such as tracks, animal homes, food that has been eaten, marks left behind, paths or trails of animals, scat, fur tufts, feathers, or bones. Dead animals (teeming with decomposing life) can also be fascinating to view (not touch). Some programs have purposely left a dead carcass in the area outside the borders of the school property (sometimes called *the beyond*) to visit on their regular trips beyond the fenced yard. The children get to see the natural cycles and changes over time.

"If you have a place with living loose parts, play there as often as you can. If not, collect them and bring them into your environment. Let your friends and family know you are collecting so they keep an eye out, too."

–Becky Gamache

Any of our outdoor classroom spaces can be transformed to include more nature and animals. The children's book *On Meadowview Street* by Henry Cole shows how a young girl notices a small blossom as her father is mowing. She develops a bond with the plant as she admires its beauty and decides she'll save this flower. She puts up a string fence around it. As she protects her small wildlife preserve, she notices another wildflower and expands her fence until it is quite large. Butterflies start to visit. Eventually, her father puts the lawn mower up for sale. The girl decides she needs a shady spot, so her parents help her get a maple tree for the yard. This process continues. Soon, the neighbors' yards start changing as well (Gull, 2015).

On a recent visit to a family child-care program in Michigan, Carla noticed one area where the grass was allowed to grow longer. Bird feeders hung from nearby posts. Under one of the trees was a stick shelter. Small posts indicated where a new tree was growing, planted from a maple samara the children found in the yard. Carla overheard one of the boys call it the "nature preserve." This was a space they knew at a young age was for

connecting to the wilder side of nature, even amongst their neighbors and sidewalks. No matter the space, we can all enhance the habitat to have our own "nature preserves" nearby, ready for children's play and inquiry-based learning.

Similarly, these same concepts can happen in urban settings and in places with Indigenous ties.

> Being in the city, we bring as much permanent nature (trees, rocks, logs, animals, gardens) as possible, but I personally source a lot of items from outside the metro area on a regular basis to keep our outdoor classrooms full of nature findings. The cabinets we have at each location are filled with supplies that teachers can use to explore in more specific ways, such as creating art with smaller nature findings or using mirrors, magnifying tools, books, silks, paints, clay, and other items that need to be put away when done.
>
> —Sara Evans
>
> In my neighborhood there were no open spaces dedicated to native plants and animals. I've purchased two parcels/lots with the intention of planting all native plants for the native animals and also at the same time honor the Elem Indians who lived, foraged, hunted, and fished here before it was developed. Finding arrowheads and spear tips in the soil spurred me to include honoring the original inhabitants of this land as I add and monitor the increasing biodiversity.
>
> —Donna Mackiewicz

THE BASICS FOR CREATING ANIMAL HABITATS

Enhance habitats for animals by growing plants that are native to your area. Native plants are the food for native insects, so when you have plants native to your space, you increase the likelihood these plants will be hosts for insects. In turn, the plants and insects attract birds. Look for local or state native plant groups. Many groups often host native plant sales and exchanges. For help understanding why to plant native plants, read Doug Tallamy's book *Bringing Nature Home*.

The National Wildlife Federation (https://www.nwf.org/Garden-for-wildlife/about/native-plants) offers advice and information about regions across the United States. Additionally, as we looked at our site, we were able to bring expert volunteers out to look at the soil and sun and give suggestions for appropriate plants. You can also find reliable advice through the US Department of Agriculture's National Institute of Food and Agriculture (NIFA) website, which shares information on the cooperative extension services available in each state (https://www.nifa.usda.gov/land-grant-colleges-and-universities-partner-website-directory?state=All&type=Extension). Cooperative extensions offer advice and resources on farming, soil and water, and gardening, among other topics.

Leave some "messy" areas. Brush piles, fallen leaves, and garden refuse are spots where insects and other animals can overwinter. When a space is too tidy, there is little natural vegetation for animals to carry out their natural cycles.

Add bird and/or squirrel feeders to the outdoor area. Child-made and commercial options can attract birds and squirrels to your space for closer observation and to supplement natural options in the winter. Consider placing these near a classroom window for easy viewing from inside. In addition to food sources, animals also need water. Adding simple water features provides what animals need and adds an additional loose part to the environment.

Creating a playground for insects in your backyard or schoolyard can be as easy as leaving some good-sized rocks, boards, or logs out on the ground. What's hiding under that rock? Pick a warm day to move it as a class to see what's been living underneath. Invite children to notice not just what scatters right away, but also bring some magnifying glasses and binoculars to wait and see what else is hiding there. As the ground warms up in the sunshine, more critters may crawl into view. This is the perfect opportunity to model patient observation and practice descriptive vocabulary: "What do you notice? What do you think? Why?"

Consider making a hotel for local insects or "minibeasts." Educator Stacey Lea Singh from Moorevilla Nursery explored minibeasts with the children: "The children had expressed the beetles might be cold, as we couldn't find many on our searches. They said, 'We need a house for them to keep warm.' We had discussions of where we find them, and what they might like. The children found a huge log and worked together to move it across the garden, [which showed] amazing teamwork [at our] preschool. We can't wait to see if we have any visitors."

If the children are particularly engaged in creating and observing native habitats, consider certifying your outdoor habitat space. For example, the Monarch Watch organization offers information on creating a monarch butterfly waystation to support these insects on their annual migration. To learn more, visit their website (https://www.monarchwatch.org/waystations). The National Wildlife Federation also has a certification process for backyards, schools, neighborhoods, and places of worship that want to create havens for local wildlife. What better way to encourage children to explore nature than through a wildlife habitat right outside their classroom? Family members, teachers, students, and community members can come together to help develop and maintain an outdoor classroom that benefits children and wildlife. The space will need food (often just native plants), water, some type of cover for animals, a place where animals can raise young, and demonstrated sustainable practices. Learn more at https://www.nwf.org/certify.

According to the Pollinator Partnership, about 85 percent of flowering plants need pollinators, and one-third of the food we eat is made possible by pollinators (Pollinator Partnership, 2024).

Pollinators include the bigger honeybees and bumblebees but also many types of smaller solitary native bees. Butterflies, birds, praying mantises, moths, and bats are also pollinators. The surprising second-most-common pollinators after bees are actually flies.

You want to make sure family members, administrators, and other stakeholders understand why it is important to help pollinators and how you plan to keep children safe. Native bees are not aggressive, but if you are worried, place habitats away from areas where children play. Try the back of a lot, beyond the fence, or by a classroom window on a different side of the building than the playground. Bumblebees and honeybees aren't usually aggressive toward humans but will protect their nests. Wasps can be aggressive, but they aren't all bad. They eat aphids that harm vegetable plants, as do ladybugs and lacewings. Usually, these pollinators will leave us alone if we leave them alone, but always supervise small children closely.

Habitats to attract pollinators include flowers that produce nectar and pollen. Look for plants native to your area, which usually tolerate local conditions better and grow deeper roots. Consider planting them in pots, raised beds, or greenhouses on your playground, and in the visible areas beyond the fence. Be somewhat messy gardeners by leaving sunflower and coneflower seed heads for the birds to eat in the winter. Pollinators also need water, so consider adding a birdbath, fountain, or shallow water dish if there's not a natural water source nearby. Good pollinator habitat can be created by leaving a leaf pile or compost pile in a corner, especially over the winter.

There are lots of DIY websites that offer plans for making native bee houses from reeds, paper straws, or small holes drilled into a chunk of log or block of wood. Pencil- or marker-sized bamboo tubes will work if there aren't too many knots that narrow the openings; bees aren't able to enlarge those to pass through. If making bee houses out of wood, drill the holes five or six inches deep. If children help with the drilling, make sure to use a softer wood such as pine, use a vice to hold the wood steady, and wear safety goggles. Pre-drill a pilot hole to keep the drill bit from slipping. Use different-sized drill bits to create varying holes that will attract different native bee species. Sand any rough edges on the openings to avoid damaging bees' delicate wings. Add a roof or overhang to help keep them dry. Keep your bee house small, with twenty or fewer holes. Solitary bees don't like crowds, and bigger houses may create a buffet for their predators.

Place the bee house in a secure location where it won't blow around in the wind, because solitary bees aren't great at landing on moving targets. Any height will work, so place them where you and the children can observe them best. Face the bee house east or south, and install it in the spring. Each year, clean out the holes or replace straws to discourage mold growth.

Set up a worm bin for vermicomposting. Worm composting can be done in many ways. When properly managed, there is no stink and the bin teems with life. You can find easy instructions online, such as on the extension and outreach website of Iowa State University (https://hortnews.extension.iastate.edu/how-create-and-use-vermicompost). The resulting compost is great natural fertilizer for local plants.

Need a little inspiration? Visit https://tylerarboretum.org/the-pollinator-preserve-at-tyler for tips and advice.

My classroom had large windows at child level and plenty of counter space. I had a paraprofessional working with me to help plan and facilitate classroom activities. We would kneel in the classroom to get an idea of a child's view of the room and consider their perspective and needs when we designed our space. The school was located in a neighborhood with many beautiful trees and plants. We had space to install a garden where we planted vegetables and flowers, which attracted insects. The empty lot behind the school had trees that attracted many birds.

—Cherry Mays

Each outdoor classroom is designed to invite safe risk taking and open-ended play throughout while also having more focused areas available for loose parts exploration. We divide each by age group, so there is a larger hill and water source for older kids, for instance. We have cabinets stocked with all manner of loose parts and binders full of provocations and schema information, should the teachers need added guidance.

—Sara Evans

My outdoor classroom space is small, but the children get to engage with the seasons. Our space is unique in that we have three large raised beds for hands-on play and exploration. With grant money, I hired a chainsaw artist to carve a log car and mushroom stumps.

—April Zajko

As noted by the contributors, each of our spaces is unique. Living loose parts can be applied in a variety of ways. What might work in your setting? What unique ideas do you and the children in your setting bring to your exploration of the natural world?

Even the most engaging teachers are no match for live animals in capturing children's attention. Encounters with animals can teach children empathy, respect for all living creatures, and self-control. Everything becomes more exciting when animals are involved. Even brief encounters spark conversations for months afterward. Photos allow children to sequence the events and practice descriptive vocabulary as they relive the experiences.

Laura once taught pre-K in a large classroom that was the former school library in a high-poverty urban school. Through monthly family meetings held inside the classroom and family members coming in the back door for pickup and drop-off, families felt at home there. Despite having limited resources, families began donating pets and supplies. Soon there were two parakeets that sang along whenever the class sang, two occasionally loud guinea pigs, a very quiet bunny, a fish tank, cocoons that later revealed butterflies, and an incubator for hatching chicken eggs. The children learned to be gentle with the animals, notice when they needed their cages cleaned, and replenish their food and water as daily jobs. They told stories about the animals and drew pictures in their journals. They helped each other understand the animals' points of view—a big step for four- and five-year-olds.

When Laura was a lab-school director, the kindergarten class proposed holding a wedding for their class hamsters. Their teacher asked what they'd learn with this project, and the children voted to write invitations and prepare snacks, which included researching what makes a healthy hamster snack. They wrote vows and music to sing at the ceremony and assigned roles for each child to be involved. Families joined them for the big day, where lasting memories were made.

> By incorporating living loose parts into our learning environments, our educators encourage children to engage in hands-on exploration and experimentation. Children are naturally drawn to living things and often express an innate sense of wonder and curiosity about the world around them. By providing opportunities for children to observe and interact with living things, we help nurture and sustain their sense of curiosity, leading to deeper learning and understanding.
>
> —Paola Lopez

CHAPTER 5

Playing It Safe: Death, Decay, and Reasonable Risk

Risk is inherent while interacting with living loose parts. Leaning into understanding risky play helps us find appropriate ways to explore our surroundings. This chapter will look at risky play in general, safety with our littlest learners, stick play, deconstructive play, safety and legal considerations with animals, and fire safety. Additionally, we'll tackle the hard topics of death, decay, and decomposition and follow up with an interview with two scientists who explore all the "gross" stuff.

"We need to let children move in ways that make adults gasp."

–*Angela Hanscom*

Assessing Risky Play

We all have different comfort levels and opportunities for risky play in our settings. By embracing risky play, along with the information, attitudes, and skills to support it, we allow children to be curious about the parameters of their bodies, negotiate risk, and interact with nature. Risky play in general promotes a variety of benefits by creating the need for:

- critical thinking,
- imagination and creativity,

- problem solving,
- self-confidence,
- social interaction,
- dexterity and physical strength,
- cognitive and emotional strength,
- resiliency,
- risk negotiation, and
- spatial awareness (Gull et al., 2018).

Many of us remember doing something as a child that might even make us gasp today. Did you ever:

- ride a bike with no hands?
- climb on the roof of a house or building?
- wrestle with a sibling?
- walk or bike to the store by yourself or with friends?
- spend time outside without your parents?
- use a tool such as a knife?

While these activities may seem extreme for younger children, they were once part of the norm of childhood.

How comfortable are you with risky play?

With many options for risky play and different categories, such as great heights, high speed, potentially harmful tools, near dangerous elements, rough-and-tumble play, and locations where children can "disappear" or "get lost" (Sandseter, 2007), we may not feel comfortable with all these types of play. There are things to consider for the children involved, such as the space and materials available and the comfort level of the educators. *Adventures in Risky Play* by Rusty Keeler (2020) can help guide you through the process of finding your "yes" for risky play, along with supporting that play through a benefit-risk analysis, the inclusion of loose parts, understanding *risk* versus *hazard*, and program examples. Engaging in risky play can encourage encountering living loose parts, such as getting closer to animals in a responsible way and taking different perspectives from the point of view of an animal while tree climbing. A tree can be considered a gigantic living loose part. In Carla and her research colleagues' academic investigations around tree climbing, we found that we sometimes limit risky play as educators because of parental concerns and/or perceived concerns. Gull et al. (2020) suggest several ways of getting families on board with risky play.

- Let parents know the benefits of risky play.
- Include risky play as part of the expectations and culture of the program.
- Communicate safety guidelines with parents.
- Host training and educational opportunities for parents around risky play.
- Share the Outside Play Toolkit to allow parents to work through various scenarios (available at https://outsideplay.org).
- Ask caregivers to be involved with risky play supervision.
- Investigate the use of risky play agreements, waivers, or permission slips.

Families can become great partners in risky play as they see the benefits and resilience of children as each child chooses to negotiate risk at their own pace.

Safe Sensory Exploration for Our Littlest Citizens

Babies and toddlers learn about the world through their senses. We want to keep them safe by observing them closely and making sure we can see and hear them at all times. Because they tend to put items into their mouths, ensure that things they explore are too large to fit inside a paper-towel tube. When you plan to give items for babies and toddlers to explore, check for any pieces that could come loose and cause choking. For wooden items, make sure they are made of unfinished wood to prevent the risks associated with toxic varnishes, lead paint, or pressure-treating. Sit with and watch young children anytime they are eating. Parents may not yet be aware of allergies in very young children, so avoid common allergens such as grass, cedar, milk, strawberries, legumes, and nuts. Watch children closely for any redness, swelling, or difficulty breathing.

Once you've chosen materials for safe exploration, there are many wonderful sensory experiences you can provide. For example, one center has a snow cone truck visit the playground monthly in the summer; older children get a sweet-syrup-and-shaved-ice treat. Teachers decided to include the babies by bringing them out in their buggies and letting them get cups of plain ice to explore. For more ideas, check out "Loose Parts Play for People Under Three: Setting the Stage" (https://home.edweb.net/webinar/classroommanagement20230523/).

Stick Play

While some educators are uncomfortable around stick play, we can build our skills and opportunities for children to constructively play with this free and often plentiful loose part in our environment. Carla often observes children using sticks to explore sound possibilities, as props in imaginary play, as math and literacy tools, and as tools for creating and building. Benefits of stick play include supporting the development of small and large motor skills, eye-hand coordination, cooperative play, creativity and imagination, problem-solving skills, risk-negotiation skills, and consideration of other people.

Based on Gull et al.'s research (2018) around tree climbing, injuries that may happen with trees and wood involve splinters, eye injury, cuts, bruises, scrapes, or impalement. These are concerns; however, they can be made less likely by using approaches to help children navigate the risk. Carla's approach to sticks includes using phrases such as "Sticks need space" and "Stick to stick" (if allowing children to hit sticks against each other). She also frequently asks, "What's your plan for safety?" If there seems to be an issue, she may redirect the child to a different activity, point out the potential safety issue, or use proximity to encourage more thoughtful use of the sticks. She also watches for and intervenes as needed in practices that could become hazards, such as running with sticks or going down the slide with a stick. When working with younger children or groups she is not familiar with, she may have a designated area for stick play, assign each teacher to supervise one particular risk, or encourage children to use sticks shorter than their forearms so they have more control.

In any situation, find what works in your space using a benefit-risk analysis to help you think through potential issues with sticks in your space and looking at stick-use policies in other programs. Julia Sappenfield, with Boston Preschool Network, explains their agreements for sticks: "In our school, sticks cannot be used as weapons, and you cannot hit anyone or any living object with a stick. And if a stick is taller than you, you need to ask a second person to help you move it. We love this last agreement because it not only teaches them how to communicate and cooperate with each other, it also gives them the opportunity to practice math in a meaningful way by comparing the stick to their own height" (n.d.).

> **"Being destructive for the child in a play context is just as much about tearing up old ideas and notions as it is about tearing up a leaf into tiny, tiny strips . . . and both should be encouraged."**
>
> –Marc Armitage **(as quoted in Tinkergarten, 2024)**

Playful Deconstructing

Consider the word *deconstruct*. It can involve tearing, ripping, crumbling, breaking, dismantling, undoing, dissolving, unraveling, crushing—you get the idea. Educators are often wary of the concept of destroying something; however, if we can embrace the concept of deconstructing, these same actions can be part of building curiosity and investigating the natural world in safe and respectful ways. Nature often recycles on its own, and our thoughtful deconstruction can assist in that process. Deconstructive play offers many benefits, such as sensory input and play, as well as building understanding and properties of materials. Nature is the ultimate destroyer and recycler. This process is an exploration of cause and effect, developing curiosity, STEM connections, flexible thinking, fine-motor skills, and emotional regulation (Gull, 2022a).

Consider the following items for deconstructive play:

- **Natural items for deconstruction:**
  - Clay (dried is okay too)
  - Seeds—milkweed, cattail, sunflower heads, dried beans in shells, dent corn, dandelions, gourds, pumpkins, sweet-gum balls, thistles, feather grass, jewelweed, and impatiens (exploding seeds!)
  - Fresh or dried herbs
  - Whole spices
  - Fresh or dried flowers
  - Fallen leaves
  - Ice, snow
  - Decomposing logs, old bark, soft wood, sticks
  - Baked egg shells
  - Kindling, tinder, pine needles, leaves, and sticks for fire exploration (if allowed)

- **Tools for deconstruction:**
  - Wooden or rubber mallets, golf tees
  - Scissors
  - Rocks, bricks
  - Mortar and pestle
  - Rasp, grater
  - Garlic press
  - Potato masher
  - Nutcracker
  - Vegetable peeler
  - Tweezers, tongs
  - Swatters

- Magnifying glasses
- Hands, feet
- Buckets, collecting bags
- Catapult, wrecking ball, trebuchet
- Playdough
- Bean bags
- Dissection kit
- Salt and water
- Matches, tin cans with holes near the bottom, heat for fire-making
- Hammers, screwdrivers, pliers

Tips and Safety Measures

1. Teach respect and boundaries as needed.
2. Take it outside—more space, less messy, and so many more benefits.
3. Reserve time for cleanup.
4. Gather materials responsibly. Use fallen items on the ground.
5. Ask for permission to deconstruct or pick parts off plants.
6. Use appropriate safety gear and procedures: safety goggles, designated space, supervision, and so on, depending on the activity.
7. Deconstruct your own creations, not someone else's work (Gull, 2022).

Autumn deconstruction exploration—what a joyful way to work on fine-motor skills, foster inquiry, and expand language skills. Children love to deconstruct and dissect natural materials. Sometimes, we as adults can feel upset by children's "destruction" and will set boundaries about how children interact with living plants. However, we know that children crave to understand their world, and taking things apart helps them understand things in a different way. Autumn deconstruction explorations are perfectly timed at the end of the growing season. When we look around the garden and yard, there are likely lots of natural materials that are at the end of their life cycle. So this invitation to play is all about exploring deconstruction or dissecting

natural materials as a way to learn more about the materials. For me, this isn't a free-for-all, as I do want to keep weeds, seed heads, and ample natural materials for our local animals to use for food and shelter this winter. But these invitations are well received by children and lead to some wonderful conversations.

The tools I offer to support children's exploration and deconstruction include mini hammers, tweezers, magnifying glasses, tongue depressors, and scissors. Children find rocks and pieces of branches on their own to try to crush the acorns, which are seemingly impossible to deconstruct with these tools. One child was determined to crack the acorns. She tried out all the tools and observed the other children who also weren't meeting with success. After a while, she found just the perfect stick in the forest. She placed her hand on each end of the stick and rocked. With perseverance, she figured out a way to apply enough pressure without making the acorn fly off the table. She kept at it, and when she heard that first crack, she squealed with delight. Peers at the table were so impressed, and others sought her advice on how she did it. These simple moments remind me of the power of play and the power of allowing children to struggle to find their own answers!

—April Zajko

Fire Engineers

Fire has been a living loose part throughout human history. Today, many children around the world use fire as a tool, making their own fires to cook food and stay warm. Adults may be concerned with the concept of "playing" with fire (as we should be). Yet, we may find that experimenting with the variables of fire-making builds engineering and safety skills using heat, fuel, and air. Sometimes, children need to feel the heat of a fire to understand how it works and the cautions that should be employed around it. We learn to make fire by actually doing it, not by watching videos of it. By "playing around" with the elements of fire, children understand its power and capacity. It takes experimentation and exploration to light and keep a fire going. We learn to be appropriate around fire by being around fire, not by eliminating it from our lives. Carla prefers allowing children to understand fire at a younger age by feeling the heat of a burning matchstick close to their fingers rather than waiting to introduce this element until they are teenagers and haven't benefited from years of small, incremental exposures. Fire-making can build persistence, problem solving, confidence, and a sense of joy in mastering new skills—all aspects of engineering.

Direct, personal experiences with fire-making help children develop a healthy respect for fire and its potential destruction and benefits. The following are suggested ages for fire-making activities; although, children with more supervised exposure to fire may have the capacity to explore fire more in depth at a younger age (Gull, 2023). Individuals may need additional support, guidance, and accommodations for inclusion in fire-making activities.

- **Age 2:**
    - Putting out a candle with a candle snuffer
    - Feeling the warmth of a fire
    - Dramatic play cooking
    - Pretend fire-making with sticks or logs, "flames" made of scarves, and a rock safety circle
- **Age 3:**
    - Sitting by a campfire
    - Cooking over a fire (with close adult supervision)
    - Putting out a candle with a candle snuffer
    - Using crayons on fire-heated rocks
    - Mark-making with cooled charcoal
- **Age 4:**
    - Striking a match
    - Lighting a candle
    - Preparing wood for charcoal making
    - Making a spark with flint and steel
    - Using charcoal for art
    - Expanding cooking options
- **Ages 5+:**
    - Making small, personal fires
    - Creating charcoal ink

- **Ages 8+:**
    - Making a wooden bowl using an ember
    - Creating the group fire
- **Ages 10+:**
    - Creating their own fire-making kit
    - Exploring additional traditional fire-making options
    - Experimenting with fire add-ons, such as orange peels and sugar
    - Trail cooking
    - Using lightweight camp stoves (Gull, 2023)

"Don't worry, and let it happen. If some behavior seems destructive, think of a way to redirect it. Outdoors, there's always a way."

–Heather Taylor

Permission and supervision are key components of safety. As adults, we also need to understand fire-making and its potential. The more experience we can gain, the better we can support the children in our care.

Of course there are safety considerations, such as having one staff member supervising fire-making and use at all times. Additionally, be sure to pull long hair and loose clothing back to avoid contact with the fire. Create a benefit-risk analysis of fire-making to understand how to lower the risk of potential issues in your space. Have materials handy to put out any fire and be ready to administer first aid if needed.

Umbrella House, a family child-care provider in Lansing, Michigan, uses fire in their program with infants through school-aged children. They have the following policy in place:

Campfire Procedures and Rules

We will use fire for heating and cooking in our outdoor fire pit. Following are the rules we will follow for everyone's safety.

- A current burn permit, issued by the township, will be on file.
- We will always call the fire department prior to starting a fire, to see if it is safe to burn.
- We will discuss reasons why it might not be safe to have a fire.
- The fire pit will be inside the fence with the gate latched.
- We will have buckets of water, a fire blanket, and fire gloves available before we start any fire.
- The area surrounding our fire pit will be kept clear of items that could be a tripping hazard.
- We will talk with the children, often, about fire safety.
- We will also talk about respecting the fire and why we use the fire for warmth and cooking.
- Shoes are always required near the fire pit.
- The children will be allowed to help build the fire.
- Once the fire is built, the gate will be latched and children will not be allowed inside the fence.
- Only adults will be allowed to light the fire.
- Children will be allowed to cook over the fire from outside the fence.
- Children will always be supervised with an adult while a fire is burning.
- The fire will always be extinguished thoroughly after we are done.

Carla shares her approach to helping children ages five and older make small, individual fires:

> I have had several groups of children, ages five to thirteen, light their own mini fires. I give the children time, a safe space, materials, encouragement, and an example for building their fire, as well as a healthy dose of safety parameters along the way.
>
> For containers, I use a smooth-edge can opener to take the tops off tin cans and use a bottle opener to make holes near the bottoms of the cleaned-out cans. These vents allow air to get to the fire. We work on the driveway, parking lot, or bare earth, clearing away flammable debris. Each child has plenty of space. The children collect their own tinder; they often find pine needles, dry leaves, tiny twigs, and bark. I show them a trick of using a cotton ball dipped in petroleum jelly. The children also collect lots of kindling (small sticks) to feed the fire.
>
> Each child gets a small box of matches. Many children have never lit a match; however, once one child "gets it," he or she often helps others. The children make small arrangements of sticks in their tin cans, leaving space for air to circulate. Tinder (including the cotton ball with petroleum jelly) is tucked in so it will catch fire. The children try to light the fire, with emphasis on *try*. This typically takes many, many attempts at first. Eventually, each child starts a small fire and realizes the fire's needs: oxygen, heat, and fuel.
>
> They put their fires out with water, dirt, or sand, focusing on safety. The cans do get extremely hot, so tongs and potholders are available. Some children celebrate by roasting a marshmallow over their own personal fire.

What a sense of satisfaction and accomplishment! It's great to see the children's confidence grow as they build fire-making skills. Fire starting and safety is learned by hands-on opportunities to understand the power of fire.

Carla held a session on this topic at the National Leadership Summit by Nature Explore and the Outdoor Classroom Project. She discussed creating a safe space to explore fire in its many forms: dramatic play items for "cooking" over a fire, charcoal mark-making and art exploration, magnifying glass paper burning, candle lighting (and snuffing), and various levels of challenge in creating one's own tiny fire. While some schools and/or licensing agencies may not allow fire-making on-site, it may be possible to offer fire-making lessons at Saturday or evening events for your families at local parks or lakes. Exploring and embracing fire as a loose part helps educators imagine the possibilities, heal old wounds and trauma around fire, and experiment and explore with fire as a living loose part.

Working with Animals

At times, educators may have concerns about what is found in the natural world. Carla has seen a director get on top of a table when a snake was brought into a classroom for a lesson. In another situation with preservice educators, a young child would not come within four feet of the worms the science education class was exploring. Children pick up on our concerns and anxieties around spiders, snakes, storms, and insects. As we address these concerns, remember that children listen to our voices. If we know we have issues with a certain animal, we might use a buddy system or bring in a guest presenter. Children quickly figure out which adult to go to who will be more interested in the roly-poly they find outside. As much as possible, model the desired behavior and curiosity, and express positive sentiments about animals and how they are important. Patty Born Selly (2014) shared an educator's comments: "One toddler teacher I know said, 'I can't stand spiders! I really don't like them. But the children I work with don't know that, and they don't need to. I try to share their excitement even if I'm cringing on the inside. I just focus on the smiles on the children's faces instead of my own fears about spiders.'"

Curious children can sometimes make adults uncomfortable. We need to assess our own assumptions and expectations, then prepare others to do the same. As an elementary teacher, I [Laura] found that the children in my class had a hard time learning to tell time on analog clock faces. They could answer correctly during a direct lesson but would forget the skill by the time there was a test. So I told them, "Quiz yourself. Whenever you see a clock with a face, figure out what time it is, then ask an adult nearby if you are right." I mentioned that plan at parent-teacher conferences about a month later, and a dad said, "I was wondering why he kept asking me what time it is. I've been saying, 'Why? Are you taking medicine?'"

Safety and Legal Considerations with Living Loose Parts

- **First, do no harm.** As we consider the prospect of "playing" with living loose parts, we don't want to harm nature or our own bodies. We need to be aware of the safety of the animals, plants, and children, including being knowledgeable of potentially dangerous plants or animals in our local area. Know the characteristics and needs of the living loose parts.
- Wash hands, wash hands, wash hands! Let's say it again: Be sure to wash hands before and after handling live animals.
- Let wild animals be wild. Observe from a distance.
- Stinging insects, such as wasps and bees, are often a concern. Practice staying calm. Often these insects are just checking us out for potential food sources. When we stay calm, the insect typically moves on.
- Remove any hazards in our direct play spaces.
- Know the plants in your area to be sure any brought into your space are safe for the children in your care. If you have a more natural area, consider removing poison ivy or other allergens or toxic plants from play spaces. Check each morning for hazards that may have washed, blown, or slithered in overnight.

- Typically, wild animals—from birds and squirrels to snakes and skunks—will leave the area when boisterous children come outside. But know the specific challenges in your area, and check local resources such as master gardeners, master naturalists, and county extension agents. For example, one preschool with a playground bordered by swampy wetlands installed a barrier made of a material that is unpleasant for snakes to cross. The material was effective at keeping the playground snake-free.
- Of course, accidents can happen. Prepare for emergencies by having an accessible first-aid kit, trained staff, and emergency numbers handy. A benefit-risk analysis can help determine how to mitigate risks and embrace the positive learning aspects of the situation. Document any issues or incidents to share with parents and for reflection.

A few documents are worthy of review in considering living loose parts and their interactions with our students:

- National Science Teachers Association: *Responsible Use of Live Animals and Dissection in the Science Classroom* (https://static.nsta.org/pdfs/PositionStatement_LiveAnimalsAndDissection.pdf)
- Centers for Disease Control and Prevention: Animals in Schools and Daycares (https://www.cdc.gov/healthypets/specific-groups/schools.html)
- National Association of Biology Teachers: *The Use of Animals in the Biology Education* (https://nabt.org/files/galleries/NABT_Position_Statement_Animals_in_Bio_Education-0001.pdf)

The NABT "strongly supports teaching which allows for student interaction with organisms, both living and dead, that provides enriched, meaningful learning experiences. The involvement of students in first-hand interactions with living animals provides opportunities for increased understanding of content knowledge, the care of living organisms, and appreciation for the value of life" (2019). Real, hands-on experiences with living loose parts enrich children's understanding of the world around them. Major takeaways from these documents include the following:

- Understanding the needs and characteristics of the animal to be included
- Learning and following local, state, national, and international regulations around animals
- Creating and following a plan to keep the animal and children safe
- Planning for responsible future care of the animal
- Considering allergies and other illnesses that may affect interaction with animals
- Washing hands before and after handling
- Keeping animals in designated areas that are regularly cleaned
- As educators, modeling respect and caring for animals

Beware of exceptions to collecting, such as leaving endangered species in the wild. If you want to collect amphibians for short-term use in the classroom, a state fishing license is often required. Additionally, in considering legal aspects of interacting with living loose parts, do not collect materials from migratory birds, such as feathers, nests, mounts, and eggs without proper educational permits as outlined in the Migratory Bird Treaty Act. (You can find out more on the US Fish and Wildlife Service website https://www.fws.gov.) Don't worry, we'll help you find resources in other chapters and appendices. At centers Carla works with, they often observe protected species in the wild and then have other options of materials for children to play with, such as craft-store feathers, chicken feathers, or realistic turtle shells made of resin.

While we have outlined some considerations, please thoroughly consider your own educational and ethical philosophies, as well as local and national laws pertaining to living things in the classroom. Create a policy for your school or setting to outline what your interactions with animals might be. For example, the Indiana Health Code suggests determining the following:

- Clarify your specific educational purposes.
- Which types of animals are allowed in your setting?
- At what times will animals be allowed in the classroom?
- How long will the animal stay in the classroom?

* Who is responsible for housekeeping/cleaning requirements?
* Determine how allergy issues will be addressed.
* Post and remind children of handwashing/contact procedures.
* Establish who is financially responsible for food, supplies, vet fees, and potential injuries.

Consider a benefit-risk analysis for animals at school. See an example at https://www.stpaulsjuniorsomerset.org.uk/docs/Matilda_risk_assessment.pdf

In the past, we might have considered the risk when making decisions about what to include in our work with children. However, Rusty Keeler, author of *Adventures in Risky Play* (2020), suggests first considering the benefits for the child and then weighing that in a benefit-risk analysis. Discuss options with your school administrator, program licensing agent, and insurance company representative. Be sure to follow local, national, and international health guidelines.

Death as a Living Loose Part

With live animals, so also comes death. Death can become a great teacher as we interact in our spaces. Insects and small animals typically have shorter life spans than humans do. In observing these creatures, children will witness nature's life cycle on a regular basis. Additionally, you will likely encounter dead animals as part of your STEM explorations outside. Rather than shying away from a dead bird, get curious. This curiosity can lead to investigation, mathematics, communication, and environmental action. Consider the following example from Megan Gessler of the Morton Arboretum in Lisle, Illinois.

> Earlier this fall during migration, our afternoon students began to notice a pattern of finding dead birds underneath a specific window. They were saddened and very curious as to what was happening. They lovingly buried the first found bird in a pile of soft leaves. Then they went back the next day with a bird guide to identify the species only to discover that the buried bird was gone! But another dead bird was below the window. Was it the same one? They painted this bird's foot and buried it to see if the bird would reappear the following day. It, too, went missing!
>
> As the children continued to find more dead birds, they hypothesized about why this was happening as they looked at reflections in the window during various times of the day. Their teachers began wondering aloud to get the children to think critically about cause and effect. "I wonder what the bird saw in the window as they were flying?" The children responded, "They see the grass and sky, but not the window!"

As our program promotes becoming agents of positive change for our natural world, the teachers then wondered aloud about how we could help the birds. The children decided to use their voices by communicating with our facility manager via their drawings. One child drew a picture of the tree and the burial plot. Another drew a picture of their sad face and a sad sun as they gazed upon the burial site. The teachers then scribed a letter asking for collision stickers for the windows.

Last week, the children were so excited to meet a facilities staff member as they learned about the science behind the UV reflective window clings, and they got to watch them being installed. How empowering! Our children felt heard and valued. I'm so proud of our educators, our students, and our facilities staff!

By noticing the issue at hand, children were able to learn about, with, in, and for nature, and to advocate for changes at the center to prevent additional bird strikes. Some even went home and created pictures to put on their own windows to protect the birds.

Some nature-based schools have created a boneyard where dead animals are left to decompose, often in a cage so the animal doesn't get carried away while decomposers still have access to it. Classes visit the dead animal regularly to observe the changes. Death is a curious topic for children. At Merry Lea Environmental Learning Center, when the children found a dead deer on the trail, they wanted to know what would happen to it over time. They made regular visits to observe and even asked if they could bring it back to their outdoor learning classroom. The teacher gently guided them in considering the odor, and the children decided to leave the carcass there. Over time, coyotes and other animals got to it, spreading parts of the animal about. With permission, children chose to drag a few parts closer to their learning space to observe and see what might happen.

Another program in the region chose to bury a dead animal they found. Later, they tried to dig it up to see what had happened, but the animal was no longer there. Where did it go? These experiences help children consider and understand the natural life cycles and food webs that happen in nature. The children's book *Vulture View* by April Pulley Sayre gives an inside look at the turkey vultures whose keen sense of smell leads them to carrion for food. Sayre shares information about the actual cleanliness of the birds and how they are part of nature's decomposers.

Death in our natural spaces can also be a time to touch on the social-emotional aspect of loss in our lives. Understanding death through creatures around us can help as children start recognizing that death happens for humans as well. Having appropriate, child-driven opportunities to commemorate a dead animal assists in thinking of memorials for our own loved ones. In one encounter, a young boy suggested having a service for a dead bird with songs and moments to talk about the animal before burying it, practices he had experienced with the death of a family member.

Children's Books on the Topic of Death

Buscaglia, Leo. 1982. *The Fall of Freddie the Leaf: A Story of Life for All Ages.* West Deptford, NJ: Slack Books.

Hill, Frances. 2002. *The Bug Cemetery*. New York: Henry Holt and Co.

Thomas, Isabel. 2021. *Fox: A Circle of Life Story.* New York: Bloomsbury.

Viorst, Judith. 1987. *The Tenth Good Thing About Barney.* New York: Aladdin.

Wise Brown, Margaret. 2016. *The Dead Bird.* Illustrated ed. New York: HarperCollins.

At Merry Lea, animal parts are always exciting discoveries to find. While keeping in mind health and safety, different animal parts (feathers, shed skins, bones, antlers, fur) can lead to exciting investigations and discovery.* We can practice fine-motor skills through cutting, tearing, and folding. We practice gross-motor skills when we carry large objects back to our classroom space. We practice social-emotional skills when we have to negotiate the use of a single find by the entire group. A few times, we have found whole or partial carcasses such as hummingbird, fox, vole, deer, hawk, rabbit, and duck. We have used these in our space to investigate different types of anatomy such as feather varieties, eyes, fur, teeth, and hoofs. We have also placed these decaying creatures under a wire cage that allowed small creatures to enter but kept the carcasses inside. (We did this a short distance from the classroom to keep the smell away.) We could visit on class days and watch the process of decay. We observed the different layers of anatomy and the different rates at which animals were eaten. For example, we discovered that ducks have really tough, water-resistant feathers that slow down eating them. We noticed the tooth marks left by small animals chewing on the carcasses, and much more. Throughout this whole process, we carefully and intentionally facilitated the necessary emotional process around death that different children experienced in different ways, keeping in mind the many varied home situations that affect this important developmental growth.

Likewise, fungi are typically helping decomposition in the natural world. Mushrooms are organisms that can be mysterious and enigmatic, even to adults. The children have noticed that some fungi change quickly, appearing and decaying within a matter of days. Others remain across years. Many notice the softness or hardness of different fungi or investigate the pores, teeth, and gills. Some engage with the unique smells of fungi that change with the weather. Spaces around fungi begin to change as moisture and season cause the mushrooms to release spores, introducing new colors and a powdery layer for drawing with fingers or other loose parts. **Safety note:** Teach children not to put anything they find outside in their mouths unless an adult says it's okay.

*Note: We have permits that allow this type of exploration. Please follow your local regulations and health codes.

A Conversation with Scientists about Gross Stuff

Andrine Shufran, PhD, is an entomologist and coordinator of the Oklahoma State University Insect Adventure. Joe Rackley is an environmental conservation educator and an Oklahoma state pest survey coordinator.

ANDRINE: Children may say, "Oh! Eww!" but I have found they actually love learning about gross things. Half of learning is keeping it in, using the information. When it's gross you remember it.

JOE: The key to what you do later in life is buried somewhere in your early life. If we avoid taking any risks, if we avoid all unsavory topics, we might not spark scientific interest.

On termite races:

ANDRINE: First you need to get termites. Let parents know: they don't bite, there's no queen, so you won't get an infestation. If they get out, they will just scatter. They won't cause damage. They are about the size of a grain of rice.

JOE: They're everywhere. Turn over a rotting log. You'll find them. Take a paintbrush to brush them into a plastic container with a lid. You don't want to put them in a cardboard box.

ANDRINE: No. You don't. Or, you can take a stake of unfinished wood. Stick it into the ground at least 30 feet from any structure. (Many buildings have been treated for termites, so you won't catch them up close to a building.) Go out about once a month and try to wiggle your stake. When it wiggles—it has termites. Dump them into your container. Then get some cheap Bic pens.

JOE: They have to be the Bic brand.

ANDRINE: There is a molecule used to make the ink flow that happens to mimic termite pheromones. Termites will follow whatever line children draw. When they draw a racetrack or write their name, connecting the letters, the termites will follow right along that line. They are creating a trail pheromone. The scent will fade after a little while, and you can talk about why they stopped following it.

JOE: You could create a scent trail for children to follow using flip-top vials or small cups with cotton balls soaked in scents like lemon, almond, or orange extract, Vicks VapoRub, or vanilla.

ANDRINE: Why does this work? Termites live in the dark. They don't talk. They need nonverbal, nonvisual communication. You can try Sharpies or other brands of pens. They won't work. The specific Bic scent is their communication tool.

JOE: You could keep your termites in an ant colony viewer, if you want.

On painting with maggots:

ANDRINE: Get maggots from a bait shop. They come in sawdust. Let parents know: they won't make anyone sick. They make their own antibiotics. It's a waxy coating on their body. They cannot bite, they only have a tiny straw-like proboscis to slurp up what's already soupy. You can watch it work.

JOE: That's why they're useful in medical applications, like cleaning wounds on burn victims. They don't take any healthy tissue or cause any harm.

ANDRINE: Unlike us, they can breathe and feed at the same time. Their nostrils are located at their bottom end so they can burrow into goop and still breathe. You want to add a little water to tempera paint.

JOE: To break the surface tension?

ANDRINE: Yes, about 19 parts paint to 1 part water. Just a little. So the maggots can drag the paint better. Just put blobs of paint on paper and add a few maggots. You can use school colors or whatever the children want. Just watch them go.

JOE: There are all sorts of opportunities for inquiry.

ANDRINE: Follow each of these activities by looking closely at the animal.

In this chapter, we've discussed things that may make some adults uncomfortable. As teachers, we make thousands of decisions every day. When we practice considering the benefits and risks of an activity, we examine the balance of protecting children and allowing safe, valuable experiences while also promoting creativity and problem solving.

CHAPTER 6

Creative Thinking and Technology Springboards

Living loose parts often spark imagination and creativity. In this chapter, we examine inspired thinking with living loose parts, divergent thinking, play residue, and technology as part of living loose parts.

Inspired Thinking with Living Loose Parts

Natural objects are bursting with inspirational potential. Humans are discovering that almost everything that exists in nature is, or was, useful for some practical purpose. When we think about what we are observing, we can draw parallels to more familiar things. For example, the humble dandelion's seeds can be carried on the wind over sixty-two miles (Brogan, 2022), farther than any other plant we know of. That's one quarter of the way to the International Space Station! Reflection can inspire us to take our ideas into uncharted territory. When a pond or tidal flat begins to dry out, the clay on the surface shrinks faster than the mud below and begins to crack in regular patterns. These cracks might remind us of the lines on our hands that become more pronounced when the surface of our skin gets dry. Observing these patterns might lead us to create a similar design with kitchen tiles or paving stones or to sketch an Escher-like drawing.

Much of science fiction draws inspiration from natural phenomena, such as monsters with insect-like features and otherworldly geographic features that mimic those of Yellowstone. Look closely at living loose parts and see what thoughts they bring to mind. Then, use words as loose parts to describe your ideas. Writing lists of words to describe a seed or rock can inspire spontaneous poetry. Sketching a bug or flower can lead to detailed drawing, which can lead to deeper noticing and comparisons. Children today have instant access to more information than they can ever learn. We don't need them to hurry up and memorize it all. We need to help them slow down and begin to construct understanding. To think, reflect, connect, and feed their natural curiosity. To think a thought that no one has ever thought before. To learn. To be creative.

Research continues to show that children use more expressive language and more creative storylines in play when the toys or props they use are less specific and more generally representative. For example, the Timpani toy study (Measimer, 2015) found that children playing with a highly-detailed cash register that made sounds chose to focus on pushing the buttons resulting in sounds, while children with a wooden block in the general shape of a cash register pretended to be shoppers and clerks and used more vocabulary associated with shopping and checking out at a store.

Curiosity and creativity flow from rich learning environments that challenge and inspire. Sometimes, a walk outdoors is all the inspiration children need. When we are passively consuming media, thoughts are flying at us faster than we can process them. We all need screen-free time to slow down, contemplate, breathe, and think. As you consider ways to enrich your environment, think about the Smithsonian collection of 154.8 million artifacts (Fthenakis, 2018). The museum itself estimates that less than 1 percent are displayed on any given day. We can take a lesson from this. Classrooms can be curated like a museum, if we can find storage space. Collections can be rotated and refreshed, so that broken items are repaired or replaced and our classroom collection does not become overwhelming and dysfunctional. Walls and shelves need room so the children can see what is available and where to put materials away. Learning to organize their thoughts and materials are skills that will serve children in life, long after they've mastered ABCs and 123s.

Supporting children's creative thinking starts with our expectations. Children will figure out very quickly if we are looking for one "right" answer to fill in a blank or if we expect them to think deeply. When we focus on one predetermined answer, children will guess at it without really thinking, or they may disengage entirely as they figure someone else will jump in with the answer and the class will move on. When we slow down our conversations, we can listen to children's perspectives and ask questions to extend their ideas. For example, instead of telling children what a tool is for, make a game of guessing. Model noticing the parts of the tool and how they are like things the children are familiar with. Ask the children to point out what's different and what the purpose of that could be. Look for variations in size, such as a home kitchen whisk compared with an industrial-size whisk from the school cafeteria.

A related creative thinking game is to write stories together as a group. Start with a prompt, such as, "One day I went walking, and I saw a ____." What happens next in the story becomes a source of joy and anticipation as children contribute details of the adventure. Researcher Vivian Paley's wonderful books detail the daily life of her kindergarten class at the University of Chicago's John Dewey Lab School, where the children's invented stories were the basis of the curriculum. *Wally's Stories* (1987), *The Boy Who Would Be a Helicopter* (1991), and many others help us see the world of kindergarten through the stories the children create. Paley's magical gift is bringing these stories to us so that we can begin to understand life through a child's eyes and hear through their creative use of language to make meaning.

How we support children's play can promote creativity. What is the role of educators in loose parts play? Caring, observant adults who support creative play and learning are an aspect of creativity. Kiewra and Veselack (2016) suggest asking open-ended questions that further scientific inquiry and ensuring long blocks of time for deep exploration. They encourage educators to be keen observers of children's play to see and document learning.

Teachers can strategically support children's processes and thinking by being close to the children, offering observations, facilitating and scaffolding children's learning, and following their lead without taking over (Veselack, Cain-Chang, and Miller, 2009). Trust the children to make decisions, and talk with them to promote taking other perspectives and learning about problem-solving (Veselack, Cain-Chang, and Miller, 2009). Further, Kiewra and Veselack (2016) and Veselack, Cain-Chang, and Miller (2009) encourage educators to model and support a sense of wonder and offer children freedom and flexibility to use spaces and materials in unintended areas or ways.

Divergent Thinking and the Experiment Quotient

Children are naturally open to thinking up possibilities; however, at times they may need permission or a spark to get started. For one season of Tinkergarten classes, we focused on the concept of Not a Stick and Not a Box, applying this to other objects, such as dirt, a bedsheet, a bowl, nature treasures, and socks. One early elementary student looked at the sock and said, "It's just a sock." However, after the invitation to imagine and explore, the sock became much more. He realized that with divergent thinking and his imagination, the sock could become almost anything. He explored the outdoor space with the sock. This initial naysayer of thinking of sock possibilities embraced the sock play and asked to take it home to extend his experimentations.

Open-ended invitations allow children to imagine possibilities and give them permission to experiment and explore with their own voice and choice. Our settings and environments affect our behavior and attitude. After attending a Maker Faire, a gathering of people who enjoy tinkering, stretching their thoughts, experimenting, and playing with ideas, I [Carla] found that my son was exuding the spirit of experimenting and exploring. At the end of the fair, my four-year-old was highly involved in experimenting with his shadow. We talk about our shadows when we're out walking, but he was almost being a contortionist to see how his shadow would change shape and size as he shrank and contracted. I saw his mind thinking and his body twisting and turning as he made sense of it all. Then, he revised his movements and started again. My almost seven-year-old was willing to try things he never had done before. He let his body experiment with awkward positions and tried to find balance. He welded his own metal sculpture (with a little help from a professional). He was willing to try! I'm so proud of these guys for experimenting, for trying. These attitudes continued to be a part of their projects as they explored science fair projects and catapults later in the week.

At the same time we attended the Maker Faire, I was teaching several different classes and concepts, such as multiple intelligences, emotional quotient/emotional intelligence, and intelligence quotient, as well as tinkering, at the college level. With these concepts floating through my mind, I went to bed and reflected on our day at the fair. I was reminded that play is learning, play is experimenting. We need open-ended experiences for our children, our schools, and ourselves. We need to be outside. Our children need to experience this world with all five (and more!) senses in all seasons.

In all of this, the experiment quotient (ExQ) emerged. In the book *Mind in the Making* (Galinsky, 2010), the premise is that if a child is praised for being smart, when more challenging activities come along, they will not have as much patience or effort in trying to master the task at hand. However, those who were praised for their effort are more willing to experiment and try. Cultivating a willingness to try is essential. How do we develop ExQ in children? in ourselves? Can we model it? What is our resiliency as we encounter new challenges or have bumps along the road of life? Are we willing to fail? Are we willing to make mistakes? What lets us have that sense of wonder and the ability to try things out and experiment? Following are some ways educators have found that ExQ in their own settings with living loose parts.

> Start with what's familiar and try it for yourself! One of the best ways for me to discover the possibilities of loose parts was to engage in play with them myself. When I became more comfortable with the idea and use of loose parts, it broadened what I considered loose parts and what I was willing to let students engage with!
>
> —Merry Lea Environmental Learning Center

> I advise careful, thoughtful, and patient observation in the field. Most children are naturally curious, natural explorers, and natural collectors, and all of those traits need to be encouraged.
>
> —Joe Rackley

> We have an area called Fallen Tree Forest, full of fallen trees. Besides the trees themselves feeling like oversized loose parts, the branches, sticks, and twigs they produce are used for various purposes, enriching the curriculum and creativity of the students.
>
> —Peter Dargatz

> Our classroom spaces cultivate the connection with living loose parts in several ways. They are designed to be flexible and adaptable, with a variety of areas and materials that can be easily reconfigured to support different types of play and learning experiences. That includes natural elements such as plants, water features, and rocks, which provide children with opportunities to engage with the living world and observe its cycles and changes. Loose parts encourage exploration and experimentation with items that can be combined and manipulated in endless ways to create new and interesting structures and creations. This approach values process over product, allowing children to engage in open-ended, self-directed play that fosters creativity, curiosity, and problem-solving skills. It provides opportunities for collaboration and social interaction, with spaces for group work and shared exploration of living loose parts. Overall, our educators cultivate the connection with living loose parts by prioritizing nature, play, and exploration, and value the unique perspectives and interests of each child.
>
> —Paola Lopez

Each of these examples shares ways to apply creativity in learning spaces and calls on educators to play around with and try things out on their own. What resonates with you, the children you work with, and the setting you are in?

Creativity and the Need for Disequilibrium

According to Piaget, (Forman and Kuschner, 1983) learning does not happen when we are comfortable and relaxed. For true learning to take place, something has to upset the status quo and cause us to reexamine what we know to be true. We may experience disequilibrium as a sick feeling in our gut. We might feel confused, frustrated, or angry. But the disequilibrium caused by the surprising or unexpected outcome does not leave us alone; we find ourselves thinking about it without planning to. Our experiences using creative thinking will help us assimilate and accommodate new information more efficiently (Hanfstingl, Arzenšek, Apschner, and Gölly, 2021).

Constructivists believe we have three choices in dealing with a discrepant event and the disequilibrium it causes:

- **Ignore it.** That will be hard to do. The more we try *not* to think about something, the more we find ourselves doing just that. This plan might work for a while, but each time we encounter a similar discrepant event, we'll think back to this one.
- **Assimilate it.** We can take in the new information and fit it into what we already know.
- **Accommodate it.** We can change what we already know and understand to fit this new information.

Once we've done one of these three things, our mind returns to equilibrium. That is, until another discrepant event throws us back into disequilibrium. We will once again feel uncomfortable until we choose one of our three options to achieve equilibration. The cycle continues throughout our journey of life.

Play Residue, Chaos, and Clutter

Loose parts and the creativity they inspire often result in a mess—at least it looks that way to the uninitiated. Play residue, or the leavings after play has happened, are evidence of the children's thinking and artifacts of creativity. Play residue can inspire innovative ideas in other learners. Consider what could be left behind after an outdoor activity or left out in the classroom as a jumping-off point for the next session. These decisions will vary by personal comfort level and the rules for the space. To plan for and deal with the residue in a way that works for you, we suggest the following:

- Examine your own comfort level. Decide where you can compromise and where you want to establish rules and boundaries.
- Reflect on how much control over the activity belongs to the children.

- Explore ways you can give them more power over their play.
- Include cleaning up as an instructional part of every living loose parts lesson and activity.
- Plan your storage options ahead of time.

Teach children the explicit steps in getting the materials out, using them without damage (unless it's a deconstruction activity), and putting them away so they are ready for the next time. Writing a sign to protect constructions they want to save is an authentic literacy lesson for children.

There is such a thing as too much stuff. If children are tripping over the loose parts or just dumping tubs on the floor instead of engaging in play, consider whether there may be too much stuff, or whether they need more guidance, inspiration, and modeling.

With so many ideas and options around living loose parts and creativity, it might feel overwhelming. As educator Paola Lopez shares, if you are exploring using living loose parts in a preschool setting, here are some tips to keep in mind:

- **Start small:** Begin with a few items and gradually add more over time.
- **Be intentional:** Be mindful of the materials you choose and how you present them. Consider how the items connect with your curriculum and the interests of the children.
- **Encourage exploration:** Give children the time and space to explore the living loose parts in their own way. Allow them to make connections and discoveries on their own, without adult direction.
- **Ask open-ended questions:** Instead of asking leading questions, encourage children to think deeply and make connections. Ask questions such as, "What do you notice about this leaf?" or "How does this rock feel?" Encourage children to reflect on their experiences and generate their own ideas and questions about the living loose parts and technology tools. Having a list of open-ended questions on hand can be useful.
- **Foster collaboration:** Encourage children to work together to explore and make discoveries. This can lead to meaningful conversations and shared learning experiences.
- **Make materials accessible:** Make sure that the living loose parts are easily accessible to the children so they can use them independently. This can help foster a sense of ownership and responsibility.
- **Embrace the mess:** Living loose parts can be messy, and that's okay! Embrace the mess and encourage children to explore and engage with the materials in their own way.
- **Make friends with technology:** Begin by introducing a few living loose parts and simple technology tools that are age-appropriate and relevant to the learning objectives.
- **Observe and document:** Observe how children interact with the living loose parts and technology tools, and document their learning through photographs, videos, and written reflections.
- **Facilitate rather than instruct:** Encourage children to explore and experiment with the living loose parts and technology tools independently or in small groups, while providing guidance and support as needed.
- **Provide opportunities for reflection:** Set aside time for children to reflect on their experiences with the living loose parts and technology tools, and encourage them to share their thoughts, ideas, and questions with others.
- **Collaborate with others:** Work with colleagues, families, and community members to integrate living loose parts and technology tools into different aspects of the curriculum and learning experiences.

Be open to exploring the infinite possibilities for providing open-ended experiences for the young and not-so-young. Remove your own agenda about how you make sense of the world and embrace how it unfolds for those that you care for. Let each person interact fully with their surroundings in a way that makes sense to them, while being safe and respectful.

—Nicole Root

Step back and observe how a child is interacting with the loose parts or what they gravitate to. Is there a schema at play? How can you, as the educator, provide more opportunities to explore that budding interest?

—Megan Gessler

Tools of Creativity

Creativity can be cultivated in many ways, through quiet and focused observation, deconstructive play, and even through taking risks and adventures. Providing access to simple materials, such as sticks or clay, can support creative learning and exploration.

STICKS

Sticks and stick-like stems, dowel rods, craft sticks, and so on are often plentiful, easily accessible in our spaces, and inexpensive or free. They also offer many options for creativity. Between the ages of two and four years, Carla's youngest son wanted sticks, lots of sticks, for his birthday and other celebrations. Sticks were his natural play toy at the time. What's the attraction of sticks? They present unlimited possibilities for adults and children alike. Sticks are almost everywhere in nature, so children have easy access. Even where there are no trees or bushes, children will pick up reeds and dry grass. In the classic picture book *Roxaboxen* by Alice McLerren, children play with cane-like ocotillo stems as sticks in the desert. Toddlers seem to love the powerful feeling of wielding anything long, from wooden spoons to yardsticks. A stick can transform into anything in a child's hands: a sword, a paddle, a baton, or a giant pencil for writing in the dirt.

To keep toddlers and young preschoolers safe with sticks, make sure the sticks are at least several inches long to prevent choking. If you bring cut sticks into your playground, perhaps after pruning shrubs, be sure to sand off any sharp ends. Most importantly, always supervise young children closely, especially when they are playing with sticks. If it feels unsafe to you or the child, redirect them to a safer choice.

Books for Stick Play

Alber, Diane. 2019. *Sticks*. Mesa, AZ: Diane Alber LLC.

Anderson, Constance. 2017. *A Stick Until . . .* Cambridge, MA: Star Bright Books.

Coxe, Molly. 1999. *6 Sticks*. New York: Random House Books for Young Readers.

Danks, Fiona, and Jo Schofield. 2012. *The Stick Book: Loads of Things You Can Make or Do with a Stick*. London, UK: Frances Lincoln.

Dickson, Irene. 2018. *Stick*. Somerville, MA: Candlewick Press.

Donaldson, Julia. 2016. *Stick Man*. New York: Scholastic.

Dougherty, Patrick. 2010. *Stickwork*. New York: Princeton Architectural Press.

Ferry, Beth. 2015. *Stick and Stone*. New York: Clarion Books.

Hegley, John. 2012. *Stanley's Stick*. New York: Hachette.

Lechner, John. 2009. *The Clever Stick*. Somerville, MA: Candlewick Press.

Pinkney, Brian. 1997. *Max Found Two Sticks*. New York: Aladdin Press.

Portis, Antoinette. 2007. *Not a Stick*. New York: HarperCollins.

Rice, Clay. 2014. *The Stick*. Reedley, CA: Familius.

Clay Exploration

Clay, part of the living earth, is a fantastic natural loose part that offers a different experience than conventional or classroom-made playdough. However, we also recognize that many educators feel intimidated by using clay—we get it!

Educators inspire us by making clay available as a play provision daily. In outdoor contexts, children can even find their own natural clay soil. It just needs to sit overnight in a bucket of water so it can be strained with a screen or cloth to remove any leaves, sticks, bugs, and debris.

Penn State Extension (2023) offers the following benefits of clay. "Children will show many parts of themselves through clay experiences:

- Approaches and reactions to a new material (imagination, steps of involvement, temperament, feelings)
- Initiative, curiosity, and problem solving
- Technique and manipulation (what they do and what skills they use)
- Physical development (small and large motor skills)
- Ideas in representational forms (connecting ideas to meaning, symbolic demonstrations)
- Expression and communication (language, literacy, and social and emotional skills)
- Interactions and progressions over time (with other people, other materials)"

Be sure to choose safe, nontoxic, or natural clay for use with children and provide supervision. Protect work surfaces and/or use individual workspaces for children. A tray or baking sheet or plastic place mat can be a useful surface. Use burlap fabric to cover a table, or provide 12" x 12" plywood boards for clay work. Offer the giant slab of clay for the whole class to investigate and explore at first, or give a small ball to each child or small group. Use dental floss or wire to cut the clay into smaller chunks as needed. As always, be sure to reserve time to play with clay yourself before introducing it. And play with it alongside the children. We need to cultivate our own curiosity with this material as well.

Keep clay stored in an airtight container, adding small amounts of water as needed. If natural clay does dry out, place a wet sponge on top and wrap it tightly in heavy plastic for a few days. If it dries out entirely, place the chunks inside an old pillowcase. Tie the pillowcase shut, and let children beat it to dust with a hammer. Then, place the still-tied pillowcase of dust into a bucket of water for several days to reconstitute it.

Reserve ample time for clay exploration with children. As Sally Haughey (n.d.) suggests, "Like other art forms, the child brings their developmental needs to clay. Let the children explore the clay and bring their own curiosity.

The clay will obey the child with great respect!" She also suggests that we don't focus on the end product. She suggests asking the following wonderings when working with clay:

What do you notice about the clay?

I wonder how it feels.

How can you get it off the big block?

I wonder how we can stick the pieces together.

What happens when you add water?

Tell me about how it smells, feels, sounds, even tastes! (Haughey, n.d)

Beyond just exploring the clay, a few skills to explore include pounding the clay, rolling clay, pressing into the clay, cutting the clay, piling the clay on top of each other, and mark-making in clay. Eventually, advance to experimenting with additional skills, such as creating clay balls, making a pinch pot, rolling a slab, and scoring and slipping clay to join pieces of it together. Simple tools to start with include sticks, child-safe butter knives, craft sticks, forks, scissors, rolling pins and cylinders with texture, cans, jar lids, and natural and found objects for stamping. Of course, you can offer professional clay tools, but one art teacher we know insists that the only tools you really need are a sponge, a small lid of water, a toothpick, and a craft stick.

Books to Explore with Clay

Baylor, Byrd. 1987. *When the Clay Sings*. New York: Aladdin.

Freeman, Anna Harper, and Barbara Gonzales. 2021. *Shaped by Her Hands: Potter Maria Martinez*. Park Ridge, IL: Albert Whitman and Co.

Greenberg, Jan, and Sandra Jordan. 2013. *The Mad Potter: George Ohr Eccentric Genius*. New York: Roaring Brook Press.

Petty, Dev. 2017. *Claymates*. New York: Little, Brown Books for Young Readers.

Pinkerton, Jenny. 2020. *Play with Clay!* New York: Penguin Workshop.

Technology with Living Things

Technology is ever evolving. While we typically think of technology as high-tech and computer-based, technology also includes any low-tech tool we use to improve our lives. Traditional tools such as sticks and rocks are part of technology, especially when dealing with living loose parts, as these examples are part of the Earth's systems. Tools help solve problems, often moving into the field of engineering as well. Tools can be created with a variety of living (or living adjacent) options.

A tool we generally carry around us is our hands. With opposable thumbs, our hands can do amazing things. They learn to make marks, twist things apart, gesture, grip things, and even make shadows and shapes. Hands can throw, squish, dig, scoop, pull, interlace, and twiddle. Hands can communicate with culturally relevant motions. Hands have the potential to tear, rip, shred, and crush things. *Hands* by Lois Elhert explores how the artist watched her parents' hands sew, paint, build, and garden while she grew up. She sees her parents' hands as tools that also communicate love, and eventually, she joins hands with them as she becomes an artist as well.

A stick is a quintessential tool. Landing a spot in the Toy Hall of Fame, the stick is versatile as a tool, plaything, and imagination spark. It can be used to dig, make marks, mash, and so much more. In the book *A Stick Until...* by Constance Anderson, the reader sees how a stick is used as a tool by various animals around the world. The stick is used as a flyswatter by elephants, a walking cane by a gorilla, a spoon by chimpanzees, bait to attract birds to an alligator, a gift in the mating process for great egrets, nesting material, and game material for a boy and his dog. Just as animals in the wild use sticks, children use sticks for games, imagination, digging a hole, and supporting plants.

Creating tools may be as simple as creating our own paintbrushes with different textures by using a wooden clothespin, stick, or craft stick. Use string, wire, tape, or a clothespin to attach natural loose parts such as feathers, pinecones, small evergreen branches, long grasses, herbs, flowers, or other plant parts. Children can experiment with different applications and make their own creations.

A mortar and pestle is another simple, classic tool used across cultures that also has a place in our indoor and outdoor environments. Potential options for grinding include herbs and spices (fresh and dry), field corn, coffee, granulated sugar into powdered sugar, chalk, rock, pigments and minerals, and other materials. You might keep a separate mortar and pestle for kitchen duty and include children in the food preparation and grinding fresh herbs for a simple lemonade bar. When choosing a mortar and pestle, consider how it grips the counter, the heaviness of the product, its durability (including that of the pestle), the size of the pestle for fitting into a child's hand and not slipping, and the texture of the inside of the mortar. We also often use a stick or stone for the pestle. Mortar and pestles can be made of stainless steel, ceramics, porcelain, stone, glass, marble, green calcite, wood, and so on. Nutting stones have multiple wells for cracking open multiple nuts at a time without them flying all over the place. Basic, simple technology that works.

At Merry Lea Environmental Learning Center, the nature-based preschool uses tools abundantly in connection with living loose parts.

SHOVELS AND TROWELS

Children notice different soil textures while digging in different places and sometimes follow up on this by using the soils in different ways. For example, they use clay to make tiny dishes and loam to mix with water to make "paint." They find plant roots, which leads to exploration of and discussion about roots' functions, exploring where roots are coming from and where they are going, and so on. They discover earthworms and other soil invertebrates. They experiment with digging holes of different sizes and depths. They bury things, such as a dead starling. They try to "plant" things, such as the Christmas trees.

PEELERS, GRATERS, AND FILES

Children notice many differences between the twigs of different tree species as they use vegetable peelers, graters, and files to remove the bark. They see color differences, notice differences in smell, recognize differences in the hardness of different species, and see differences in the inner pith of the twigs. They also notice differences between freshly cut twigs and branches and long-dead ones. Some children have been using the peelers to create people out of short sections of branches.

SCISSORS

Children use scissors to cut grasses and other plant stems growing right across the trail from the opening of our outdoor classroom. They then use the materials to build structures, measure things, use as paintbrushes, make magic wands, and fasten other things together (used like string). They have used scissors to cut up feathers they have found on the ground. In the process, they notice differences in the textures of different parts of the feathers.

They have, with our permission, used scissors to cut feathers and fur from freshly dead animals we have found. They have also used the scissors to cut open parts of the animals to discover what is inside, how their parts fit together, and so on.

DIGITAL TOOLS

Paola Lopez shares that, at Kinderoo Academy, many of the tool options are digital, allowing exploration of living loose parts in a different way. The educators and children create habitats indoors, provoke interaction, and play with light, shadows, color, and loose parts. For digital tools, Lopez and her team suggest the following:

- **Nature apps:** There are many apps available that can help children explore and learn about the natural world, such as identifying plants, animals, and insects. For example, iNaturalist and Seek by iNaturalist are apps that use image-recognition technology to identify plants and animals.
- **Digital landscapes or virtual field trips:** Technology can allow children to virtually explore natural environments they may not otherwise have access to, such as national parks or wildlife preserves. Teachers can find and review videos on YouTube, NatGeo Kids, PBS Learning Media, and the National Park Service, among other websites.
- **Cameras and microscopes:** Digital cameras and digital microscopes can allow children to observe the natural world up close and capture images of what they see. These images can then be used for further exploration and discussion when projected through a digital projector onto a wall, laptop, or smart device.
- **Document camera:** A document camera can be a powerful tool for sharing images to support play with living loose parts. For example, a document camera can be used to capture detailed images and video of natural objects and phenomena. This allows children to closely observe the natural world and gain a deeper understanding of it. A teacher and children might use a document camera to capture a close-up

view of a butterfly's wings or a spider's web, and then display the image on a screen for close research. By combining loose parts with a document camera, children can explore and manipulate these objects in new ways. For example, children could use the document camera to examine the patterns on a leaf or the texture of a rock, and then use loose parts to create art or structures inspired by what they see.

- **Laptop or smart devices:** A laptop or tablet can be used to access information and resources about the natural world. Children can research plants, animals, and the environment, and learn about their characteristics, habitats, and interconnections. This information can then be integrated into loose parts play, such as building habitats for animals or creating imaginary ecosystems. A laptop can be used to document and share children's loose parts creations and experiences. Children can take photos or videos of their creations and share them with others, such as class friends and family members. This can foster a sense of pride and ownership in their work and encourage further exploration and inquiry. With older children, a laptop can be used to facilitate communication and collaboration between children and their peers, educators, and other experts. Children can share their ideas, thoughts, and questions about the natural world with others, and receive feedback, guidance, and support. This can help to build connections and relationships between children and the natural world, as well as between children and others who share their interests and passions.

- **Overhead projector:** An overhead projector can be a powerful tool for supporting play, learning, and connection to the natural world when combined with loose parts. For example, the overhead projector can be used to cast shadows of natural loose parts, such as leaves or branches, onto a wall or screen. Children can use these shadows to create art, tell stories, or explore concepts such as light and shadow. Loose parts such as leaves, rocks, or shells can be placed on the overhead projector, allowing children to examine them in detail and observe their unique features. This can encourage curiosity and a deeper connection to the natural world.

  The overhead projector can be used to project images of nature, such as a forest or a beach, onto a large screen or wall. Children can then use loose parts to build and create within this projected environment, working together to develop their ideas and understanding of the natural world.

- **Flashlights:** Flashlights and loose parts can provide children with endless opportunities for play, learning, and connection to the natural world. Flashlights and loose parts can inspire children's imaginative play. They can create stories about creatures of the night, explore the shadows and shapes, and use the loose parts to construct their own worlds. Using flashlights and loose parts can help children develop their scientific thinking and inquiry skills. They can observe and investigate how light interacts with different objects, explore the properties of materials and textures, and discover cause-and-effect relationships. Overall, flashlights and loose parts provide children with a fun and engaging way to explore, experiment, and learn about the world around them. They can promote creativity, critical thinking, and a sense of wonder and awe for the natural world.

- **Digital turntable:** Using a digital turntable or a lazy Susan allows children to see natural materials from multiple angles and perspectives, enhancing their observation and critical thinking skills. They can also use the turntable to create their own interactive stories and scenes with loose parts, further encouraging their creativity and imagination.

- **Digital drawing tablet:** Digital drawing tablets can be used to draw natural materials such as plants, animals, and landscapes. Children can then use loose parts such as sticks, stones, leaves, and flowers to create 3-D representations of their drawings. This process encourages observation, exploration, and creativity. Children can also use digital drawing tablets to draw elements of nature and then combine them with loose parts to create hybrid creatures or landscapes. This approach promotes imaginative play and can help children develop a deeper appreciation for the natural world.
- **Documenting natural phenomena:** Digital drawing tablets can be used to document natural phenomena such as weather patterns, changes in the seasons, or the growth of plants. Children can then use loose parts to create physical representations of these phenomena, which can deepen their understanding and connection to the natural world. Digital drawing tablets and loose parts can be used to support collaborative learning experiences. For example, children can work together to create a digital drawing of a natural scene, and then use loose parts to build a physical representation of that scene. This approach promotes teamwork, communication, and problem-solving skills.
- **Light table:** A light table can provide a unique and engaging way for children to explore and connect with living loose parts. The use of a light table and living loose parts can encourage children to explore the textures, colors, and patterns of natural materials in a new and exciting way. Children can investigate the parts of a flower, the details of a leaf, or the properties of a stone on the lighted surface.

These are just a few examples of the many tools and loose parts we use at our school that can support play, learning, and connection to the natural world. By using natural materials as loose parts, children can deepen their connection to the natural world. They can examine the textures and colors of leaves, twigs, and stones, investigate the sounds of nature, and learn about the natural habitats of different creatures, the properties of different materials, the cycles of nature, and the interconnectedness of living things in their environment.

The National Wildlife Federation (Coyle, 2017) suggests that apps for use outside should:

- activate the senses and expose the child to natural beauty.
- focus on animals in nature.
- help children feel safer in interacting with nature.
- encourage physical activity.
- foster nature adventure scenarios by sparking children's imaginations.
- connect close-knit social groups to help children share their experiences.
- Provide for caregiver roles so adults and children can engage in exploration together.
- Extend the experience by encouraging games, creation of natural hiding spaces, and more.
- Collect and store observations so children can bring their outdoor experiences indoors.
- Support children in learning how to use the technology's features, such as sound recording, geolocation, photography, and so on.

Be aware of children's safety when using technology. For example, be aware of geotagging on photos, avoid sharing locations, and check privacy settings. Know and monitor whether children will have contact with others. Technology provides many opportunities to enhance our time outdoors, bring nature indoors, and investigate living loose parts; however, it should be carefully chosen to support rather than supplant our connection to nature. Put the apps and technology away as needed.

Carla uses technology regularly to assist in time outside. She recommends the following helpful tools and apps:

- Weather apps: Weather Bug, The Weather Channel
- All Trails: offers information on local walking and nature trails
- Compass and maps
- Digital Camera, Digital Videos, Voice Recordings
- Podcasts: Loose Parts Nature Play, The Outdoor Classroom, The Forest School Teacher
- BigMagnify: helps children see detailed features
- Flashlight

- Make bird lists, note observations: Notepad, 1000 Hours Outside
- Calendar
- Group scheduling and communication: Group Me, Remind, Facebook Groups
- Timers: manage time effectively: "Let's try it for 15 minutes."
- Class apps: HiMama, SeeSaw, Storybook
- Google Earth: look for green spaces
- GPS trackers
- Search engines
- Identify species and plants: Merlin Bird ID Seek by iNaturalist, PlantIN, PictureThis, PlantMe
- Identify stars, planets, and constellations: Skyview Lite
- Games to play outdoors (gamification): Pokémon Go, Geocaching
- Outdoor safety apps: First Aid—American Red Cross, Offline Survival Manual
- Emergency calls (in the United States and Canada, as well as some other countries): 911

Other technology to consider include virtual reality AR devices, trail cameras, nest cams, GoPros strapped to children's heads to explore the outdoor space through their perspectives, portable metal detectors, drones, and solar cars.

Additionally, she follows different nature-related groups on social media to enhance her own nature understanding. Additionally, the groups can be a source of networking, connection, and collaboration. While these are Indiana-specific groups, let them inspire you to find regional groups that may be helpful in your situation:

- ICAN Learn Outdoors
- 1000 Hours Outside Indiana
- Various Regional Nature Play Groups in Indiana
- IN Nature: appreciation of nature, conservation ecology, and natural sciences
- Birding in Indiana: some county groups as well
- INPS: Indiana Native Plant Society
- Indiana Mushrooms: The Hoosier Mushroom Society
- Hoosier Herpetological Society

Creativity comes in many forms, such as the tools we use, divergent thinking, attending to play residue, and taking time for play and creativity ourselves. Giving tools and permission for creativity within our classroom spaces embraces the needed time and room for the process of thinking in imaginative ways. Additionally, as we ask good questions and assess learning, we support children in the next steps of creativity and interacting with living loose parts.

CHAPTER 7

Asking Good Questions and Assessing Learning

Careful observation helps us notice what the children are interested in. When we listen to their conversations and reflect on their ideas, an image of children's thinking emerges. We can support children's thinking by asking questions to help them clarify what they are wondering about. A good question is the beginning of an investigation.

In the beginning, children will need concrete support, but with practice, you will find yourself asking fewer questions as the children take over that role. Good focus questions cannot be answered with yes or no. *What* and *how* can lead us to *why*:

- What would happen if...?
- How can we...?
- Why do you think...?

Posting signs with good questions around the classroom and playground will invite visitors to engage with children and begin to understand the purposes of their play. Even children who are not yet reading benefit from environmental print that serves an authentic purpose. They will begin to see that writing is talk written down, as they begin to understand the permanence of print. A written word is the same every time someone reads it, no matter who reads it. Laura's former professor Windsong Hwu used to say, "A good question is better than an answer." He meant that questions open possibilities, while answers complete a thought or end a conversation.

Living Loose Parts Invitations with Curricular Ties

Consider the following examples, and then try a few with the children you work with. For each example, ask the children questions such as, "What is happening?" "Why do you think that happened?" "What would happen if...?" "What else can you try?"

- **Flashlights:** Place a flashlight in a dark corner. Provide a variety of translucent, transparent, and opaque objects for the children to explore. Invite the children to shine the light through fabric, plastic, and other familiar and unfamiliar objects. Ask them about what they notice with different materials.

- **Ants:** When you see ants outdoors, ask the children, "Where are the ants going?" Provide bits of leftovers from snack or lunch, and place small amounts on the sidewalk or playground. Invite the children to notice how the ants respond. Ask the children questions such as, "I wonder what would happen if we put food in different spots. What do you think the ants will do?" Try placing food in shady, sunny, dry, and damp spots. Check back throughout the day. Count the number of ants at each piece of food. Try again in different weather.

- **Earthworms:** Dig earthworms or buy some at a bait shop. Invite the children to wonder: What do earthworms like? Line half of a clear plastic shoebox container with black construction paper. Leave the other half unlined. Put soil in the container, and add the worms. After a while, ask the children, "Where did they go?" Earthworms will instinctively move toward the darker area in the lined part of the box. Have children gently find the worms with their fingers, pencils, or chopsticks. Ask the children, "Why do you think the worms did that?" If the weather is warm enough, try taking the worm activity outdoors. Children can add the earthworms to your garden or compost pile after the lesson. However, please exercise caution when releasing anything into the wild. Laura recalls an unfortunate incident when all the kindergartens in town released land snails after a study, and local gardens were overrun.

- **Goldfish:** Did you know that it's pretty easy to train a goldfish? Get a fishbowl or aquarium so you can provide a home for a class fish. Make fish feeding a class job each day. Model metacognition—thinking about thinking—for the children. For example, wonder aloud, "What do goldfish expect?" Ask the fish feeder to feed at the same spot for a week. Maybe mark the spot with a sticker. Then switch spots. Ask the children what they notice about the fish's behavior. Ask them why they think so.

  Another option is to shine a flashlight on the water just before feeding for several days. Then just shine the light at other times of the day (without pairing it with feeding). Invite the children to notice the fish's behavior. Does the fish come to the same spot where it has been fed the past few days in anticipation of feeding time? Does it come to the top of the water when it sees the flashlight, whether it's feeding time or not? Ask the children what they think about the fish's behavior. As an extension, try talking to the fish before feeding. See if children have other questions that you can help them investigate.

- **Plants:** Place some plants in sunny windows, and place others on darker shelves. Invite children to notice how the plants are growing over time. Model curiosity by wondering aloud, "What do houseplants prefer? I wonder what would happen if . . ." With a small group of children, discuss what they already know about house plants. Create a chart of their ideas and questions. Think about ways to investigate those questions. You may choose to move some plants to different areas of the room. Provide blank notebooks to the children where they can record their ideas (even if their writing and drawing are not yet recognizable to you). Revisit their observations over time. Talk about the changes you observe and brainstorm possible causes. Try new experiments as you develop new questions. Expand the exploration by comparing different plants.

* **Weathering:** We can observe changes in living things and on the living Earth. Place a chunk of brick or hardened clay under a downspout outdoors. Invite the children to examine the clay after rain, under snow, and when frozen in ice. Notice how it changes over time. Talk with small groups about what they observe and what they think is causing the changes. Look for erosion and other signs of weathering elsewhere on your school grounds. Expand the exploration with different objects.

OUTDOOR LEARNING CENTERS

Even recess provides opportunities to observe children's learning. Some states now require that recess—once synonymous with free play—also include direct lessons or optional learning center activities planned on the playground for preschool, pre-K, and kindergarten. We are not proposing that outdoor direct teaching replace the open-ended exuberant freedom of recess, but you might consider adding choices with loose parts props that scaffold children's social and academic development in interesting ways. Being in the open air brings sensory immersion of sound, sight, and touch. We might expect the visual, auditory, and tactile feel of nature to be overwhelming and distracting, but many of us find natural input calming, especially when we are free to focus where our interests take us.

Many informal education programs, such as those at parks, zoos, and aquariums, already offer academic content through playful delivery in outdoor settings. Some lessons naturally lend themselves to outdoor settings, such as making collections and sorting them. If you don't believe every preschool child is a collector, check their pockets, backpacks, and cubbies. You'll find all sorts of curated collections, from rocks and sticks to cars and candies. Comparing the sizes and colors of different leaves and flowers calls upon math skills. Science helps us identify common names and notice seasonal changes such as fall leaves and the decomposition of a pumpkin left outside as fall turns to winter. Nature walks can help sharpen all our senses while building observational skills. "You hear a bird? Where do you think it is?" "Oh look! A butterfly!" "What do you see?"

Traditional indoor activities add adventurousness when brought outside. A construction center can get louder with hammering that does not bother the class next door.

Reading on a blanket under a tree instead of on the group-time rug adds sensory experiences of the breeze, bird song, and blue sky. Bringing the easels outside adds a whole new dimension to the big-body movements of painting. A table and chairs outdoors allow drawing, a snack center, or even Lego play. In fair weather, children may rest better with their cots under the trees. Some programs are repurposing outdoor storage buildings as book sheds, art huts, dramatic play stages, and math shacks—with materials stored outside, protected from the weather and more accessible when children come out to play. Teachers do not have to haul everything from the classroom each day.

Assessment

Questions about what the children are learning lead us to assessment. Assessment allows us to document what children are learning, ensure academic growth, and plan future activities.

These checklists, photos, recordings, and anecdotal notes give you a chance to step back and reflect on each child individually and on the group as a whole. The information that you've gathered can be used to fill out progress reports and can inform daily conversations with families. Knowing each child's developmental progress will help you plan activities that are "just right" for them: not so hard that they are frustrating and not so easy that they are boring.

Effective assessment doesn't need to be a formal test or even involve paper and pencil.

- **Photos:** The children can become involved in their own assessments by taking photos of their work and then recalling their prior learning by talking about the photos individually or in small groups. For example, you might ask: "What were you doing here?" "What would have happened if . . ." "What do you still wonder about?" The photos can be sorted into digital portfolios or printed into collections for each child to share with their family.
- **Time samples:** These are created by noting at regular intervals who is working in what area. You might make a chart with each child's name and decide to check every fifteen minutes for an hour or two. Then, just make a check mark beside each child's name in the column for the activity they are currently engaging in at that specific time.
- **Event samples:** These are similar to time samples, but instead of checking in every few minutes, you will record each time you observe a specific behavior. For example, you might watch for and make a check mark on your class chart each time you observe a disagreement or children building a structure. Event samples can help you look objectively at what's happening over time.
- **Language samples:** These show growth in a child's vocabulary and thinking over time. As you are observing children work, note what they are doing and write exactly what they are saying at that moment. Spontaneous language samples can be written down as you hear them or can be recorded. Some teachers leave a recorder out and listen later to what the children were saying across the room or playground. Just make sure children, families, and your administrators are aware and understand the purpose of the recordings. As with the photos children can be an active part of the assessment by

listening to the previous day's recording and talking about what was happening. This can help develop concepts such as first/next and beginning/middle/end.

- **Anecdotal notes:** Simply carry a pad of sticky notes in your pocket. I [Laura] like to place them side-by-side in a folder and then stamp the date on each square. I write one observation for each child each week, then transfer the notes to individual children's folders. When I'm ready to complete a more formal assessment or conference with families, I have a collection of personalized observations for each child at my fingertips. Another teacher I know writes a line for each child on a piece of copy paper on a clipboard each day. At the end of the day, he cuts the paper apart by child and drops each strip into a folder for that child.

Time samples, language samples, event samples, and notes can be done weekly, monthly, or as often as you like. Observation also allows us to see, reflect on, and gather stories of the children's thinking and learning. These anecdotes can be used informally to connect with families, to extend the child's ideas, and to share our practice with other professionals. We can prepare checklists of the skills we're tracking for a quick assessment. There are lots of ways to record observations, including making audio and video recordings ourselves or giving the children a tablet to record themselves. This documentation allows us to revisit lessons. Children will enjoy watching themselves while making reflective comments on their own thinking. When bite-sized assessment is integrated as a normal part of each learning day, it won't feel like an overwhelming chore when it's time to complete progress reports. Authentic assessment improves classroom behavior by helping teachers tailor activities to better meet children's developmental needs, so they are not bored or frustrated. Assessment improves communication between adults and children through focus and joint attention and can let families know that we know and care about their child's abilities and interests.

Document the learning, curiosity, and exploration and share it via your preferred method of communication that works for the families in your program: social media, an app such as HiMama or SeeSaw, a private group chat, email, or text messages.

Asking good, open-ended questions with answers even we don't know already leads children to think more deeply about their observations and to plan their own investigations. Good questions can come from experiments that we set up or sparked by unplanned events. Pay attention to what the children are noticing and follow their lead. This close observation helps us document children's thinking and learning. The documentation allows us to notice trends over time and to plan more appropriate lessons.

CHAPTER 8

Branching Out with STEM

Science, technology, engineering, and math—nature provides inviting opportunities for all of these! In this chapter, we present practical activities to help children think like scientists, engineer like beavers, and implement math tools using loose parts and nature play indoors and outdoors.

Praxis Means Theory into Practice

Everyone is a theorist at some level, but we're not always aware of our theory-making and the ways it affects our behavior. For example, my everyday actions are influenced by my working theories about the responses I expect from other people: in traffic, when cooking for my family, and in teaching. Merriam-Webster defines *praxis* as "the practice of an art, science, or skill or the practical application of a theory."

Our personal theories of learning affect how we view children's work and behavior. Thinking about how the wheels are turning in each child's head helps us plan ways to extend their thinking through the materials we put out and the questions we ask, as well as the way we answer their questions. Do our words and actions inspire further exploration, or do we shut curiosity down? We have theories about what the children will get excited about and what they might ignore. Observing their actions helps us plan our next teaching steps. Reflecting on our own ideas as well as the meaning of the children's words and play improves how we put theory into practice with each lesson: our daily praxis.

Sometimes, educators might feel nervous about incorporating science, technology, engineering, and math lessons with young children. They may think, "What if I get it wrong? What if I oversimplify concepts or accidentally make things harder for children to learn later in school?" Don't worry if you mess up. Mistakes are a recognized part of the scientific process. Mistakes tell us what doesn't work. The most important mindset we can instill in ourselves and children is a curious approach to the world. When children are continuously learning, it matters less what we teach and more how we approach learning. When we get something wrong, we can model how to fix it. We can show children how to find reliable sources—from using .gov and .edu websites to consulting trusted experts to visiting libraries to check for accuracy. We can show them how to cope when we make a mistake or discover facts that contradict our current understanding. We can practice and model an openness to new perspectives so we can continue learning our whole lives. This will help children see themselves as lifelong learners, too.

STEM and Loose Parts

Living loose parts are naturally immersed in STEM. Educators' praxis means being intentional about planning, making connections between ideas, and helping the children build their current understanding to the next level. STEM learning is found in human and other animal habitats, opportunities for math with measuring and comparing relationships between objects, as well as the architecture and engineering involved in creating structures and classifications: things with wings, things with scales, things that are orange, and so on.

What does living STEM exploration look like with young children? Science is understanding evidence through observation. Science allows us to answer questions. When children notice phenomena such as light sprinkles followed by heavy rain or observe a kitten's claws retracting, we can restate what they've observed and help them to form good questions. Then, we can help children seek answers to those questions through observation or experiments.

- Technology is using knowledge to invent tools that we want and need. A tool can be as low-tech as a fork or as high-tech as a spaceship. With young children, technology can mean using digital cameras to record their work creating habitats for earthworms, then discussing and building upon their ideas based on what they noticed when looking at the photos they took. It can mean using software to manipulate those images to express their ideas.

- Engineering is using math and science to solve problems. Children gain confidence when we create environments where they solve their own problems. When children see a problem, we can support their ideas and help find materials to solve it. For example, if the guinea pig's cage door isn't staying latched, we can ask children to generate ideas: maybe a pipe cleaner or paper clip could hold it, or bending the malfunctioning latch could fix it. We can encourage children to observe over time to see if further modifications are needed. Did the solution work? What else could they do?

- Mathematics is much more than adding and subtracting. Even young children can notice relationships as they compare, change, and combine shapes, weights, and structures. Children might notice that rain puddles are disappearing on the playground in the hot sun. They can use sidewalk chalk to mark the edges throughout the day and lengths of yarn to compare the measurements around the edge of the shrinking pool.

Math, science, engineering, and technology give us tools to care for our planet and to learn to live with nature in more sustainable ways.

Play as STEM

Children don't separate play into science, technology, engineering, and math, yet all are prominent when children play. All academic areas are intertwined seamlessly. Giving children choice and voice in how they interact with materials allows freedom to explore, innovate, and create. Give them ample time for play and watch for the STEM concepts that emerge. While we share examples within each of these disciplines, the reality is that, when it comes to play, none of it is "tidy" within a category—STEM abounds! Our job is to observe the play, recognize the concepts that children are developing and beginning to internalize, and offer ideas and materials that extend their thinking. When you are ready to take things to the next level, consider supplementing your current habitat with some of the following options.

LIFE SCIENCE

X-rays provide an entirely new way of looking at things. They allow us to see what was formerly invisible. Families may be willing to share old X-rays and might even be willing to explain the injury. X-rays of seashells, plants, and animals are also available online. The process of creating these images may be too abstract for very young children to understand, but you can demonstrate by pointing out formerly invisible things. For example, open a peach to reveal the pit inside, or ask them to take off a shoe to reveal the foot inside.

ENGINEERING WITH THE ELEMENTS

Engineers solve problems. They look at a situation and figure out what needs to happen, often using technology, math, and science in a multidisciplinary way to make things work. John Spencer (2018) explores the role of play in engineering, referring to an unending cycle of play, curiosity, experimentation, and creativity. He argues that nature is one of the best places for these engineering activities and suggests we make nature more accessible in schools, make time for children to play frequently, learn the art of observation, apply insight from nature into the research process, and cultivate curiosity through student-led questions and inquiry. He posits, "It's not about preparing students to be engineers. It's about helping them learn to think like engineers. There's something powerful that happens when they can look at the natural world with a sense of awe, wonder, and curiosity and then connect those ideas to new designs that solve real-world problems. When this happens, they learn to think differently and ultimately grow into problem-solvers and creative thinkers."

Children can experiment with engineering with plants by using indoor and outdoor greenhouses, cold frames, root viewers, hydroponics/aquaponics, and rooting plant cuttings in water. Children can observe the plants and conduct experiments by altering the amount of water, soil, and sunlight the plants receive. Lunch scraps can be sorted into what is compostable and recyclable. Laura's local food bank suggests involving children to aid the decomposition process for spoiled fresh fruits and vegetables by putting on rain boots, adding the fruits and veggies to a trash can, and stomping them before placing them in the compost pile. (They did caution that medium-sized trash cans work better than 5-gallon buckets for this activity because children tend to stomp the bottoms out of the buckets.) If your program makes a compost pile, consider adding worms for more engineering possibilities through vermicomposting.

ANIMAL ARCHITECTS

Animals can be great inspiration for engineering play. Consider the instincts animals have to build shelter and the various methods they use to construct with natural items. Animals might be building homes, attracting mates, or attracting prey as they build. Carla provides outdoor education to local preschools, where the children often learn about animals in the area and their amazing building skills. They then try to build like the animals do.

Beavers

Beavers use mud, branches, and logs to create dams and lodges. Carla invites the children to learn more about the animals' skills by exploring wood chewed by a beaver, looking at a beaver skull replica, and feeling their fur (using one of her loose parts nature play kits). She brings in a variety of materials and building sets, such as clean, smooth tin cans; large, hollow blocks; STEM loose parts sets; straw building sets; smaller blocks; and large sets such as the NudelKart Rover. The children use the materials to engineer their own spaces. *I'm Done!* by Gretchen Brandenburg McLellan can be a great start to this nature and engineering play as it follows a young, playful beaver who hastily finishes work to play with animal friends. His parents inspect the work and encourage him to do better. When he puts in the needed effort, he is proud of his work and can play more freely. The book is filled with great onomatopoeia words for a fun read-aloud.

Spiders

After looking at the many types of spiderwebs and searching for webs in your outdoor spaces, give children small balls of yarn or craft sticks wrapped with yarn to experiment with weaving and web-making. They can cover the fences, climbing structures, benches, and other spaces in the playground in yarn as they weave like spiders. *Seaver the Weaver* by Paul Czajak is a good read-aloud, following a misunderstood orb weaver who uses the night sky for inspiration in building his webs. As other spiders notice that his triangles, squares, and hexagons actually catch mosquitoes, they branch out from building their traditional circular webs.

Nest Building

Encourage the children to use what they find in the area (sticks, leaves, moss, mud, and so on) to create their own nests, from large osprey nests made of sticks to "lazy" wild turkey nests scraped in the soil and a few leaves tossed on top. Carla has added a large collection of wooden eggs for the children to use with their nests and play. If enough loose parts and materials are not available on-site, Carla brings in a large tarp and bags of materials, such as pine needles, sticks of varying sizes, leaves, rocks, and more, for children to build with. *Mama Built a Little Nest* by Jennifer Ward is a rhyming book exploring the many ways birds make nests, including a tiny cobweb and lichen nest, a hole in a tree, a nest floating in the water, a bare nest on a ledge, birds who let someone else take care of their eggs, and many more. *A Nest Is Noisy* by Dianna Hutts Aston shows many animals that make nests. There is a simple, poetic way to read the book or a more scientific approach with detailed information and illustrations to see how birds, reptiles, insects, fish, mammals, and amphibians build their nests.

Additional Books on Animal Architecture

Knowles, Laura. 2018. *We Build Our Homes: Small Stories of Incredible Animal Architects.* Redfern, NSW: Australian Geographic.

Nassar, Daniel, and Julio Antonio Blasco. 2015. *Animal Architects: Amazing Animals Who Build Their Homes*. London, UK: Laurence King Publishing.

ENGINEERING A BUG ZOO

Engineering crops up easily in children's play, as noted by Crystal Harrison from Playful Solutions Preschool, after the children discovered a living animal in their outdoor space.

> The Bug Zoo began with the discovery of a giant roly-poly, and the kids were immediately fascinated.
>
> "Let's build a playground for it!"

"Okay! First we need to build some walls, so it can't get out. Quick! Grab the chalk!"

"He's still trying to get out!"

"I found him in the mulch. I think he wants mulch."

"And grass! Maybe he wants to eat!"

"He's trying to go be with his family! We need to find his family!"

"I have a teeter-totter for them!"

"Maybe they would like a swimming pool! Can roly-polies swim?"

The next day, I provided several books about bugs, bug-catching tools, a small bug habitat, magnifying glasses, and tape measures.

The children discovered that roly-polies have armor to protect themselves against predators. *Jake, who had been researching castles, made a connection between the armor of the roly-poly and the defenses built to protect castles. He suggested they incorporate turrets and lookout towers into their habitat designs. The children's ideas all came together in one collaborative prototype.

This habitat had all the amenities a roly-poly could want, including slides and a zipline so they could reach their food faster. However, the children who had been researching roly-poly diets began to question the use of unnatural materials.

"The birds will see the bright colors and fly down and eat them!"

"The magnets are slippery. I don't think the roly-polies can hold on."

"This book says they like to dig under the dirt to hide. We don't have any dirt!"

After gathering dirt and rocks from around the property, we went out into the neighborhood in search of different types of tree bark, sticks, and leaves.

Based on everyone's research, *Matthew drew up the final plans for the roly-poly habitat, and everyone worked together to bring the vision to life.

The children placed the habitat under a windowsill to protect the roly-polies from rain and birds. Over the next two weeks, they repurposed a box as a bug trap. They tested out different kinds of leaves and rotting wood to see what would attract the most bugs. They also built a centipede habitat for the official opening of the Bug Zoo.

---

*Children's names have been changed to protect privacy.

Watershed Engineers

Humans have manipulated water for thousands of years. Playing with water helps children understand how water flows, how it is used for transportation from one place to another, and the properties and characteristics of water. Water is a precious resource, so having a limited amount of water for play each session may work best for your space. OneFamily Home Childcare uses a rain barrel to catch the water runoff from the roof. The barrel, which has an easy-to-use spigot, is situated right by their mud spot and can be used to flood the space for puddles or to carefully fill a small pitcher. Carla often uses old water jugs and dispensers, so children older than two can self-serve water with little help. When the water is gone, the water is gone, helping conserve this resource rather than having unlimited water from a hose.

You might consider giving thanks for the water that is to be used. Rodenburg (2022) offers these suggested words of gratitude, "Most of our bodies and most of the world are made of water. It is the liquid of life. To water, who tumbles over rocks in a frothing torrent, who can hold the color blue in a lake or ocean unlike anything else. To water, whose form can change from rain to a frozen puddle, from a hexagonal snowflake to a glacier, from a dancing stream to a deep ocean—we thank you, Water, for bringing life to us and all living things."

David Sobel (1996) suggests the following for learning more about water: "The water courses of the landscape are the circulatory system of the living earth, and we can only learn them by following them, literally and metaphorically. The concepts and content of the water cycle are teachable and accessible, but only with a raft of tangible, concrete experiences to carry us through the process." Additionally, he advocates following a creek or stream to see where it takes you as you investigate and learn more about how water flows in our region. Having special places in nature where children can divert, change, and experiment with water flow gives them practical experience with understanding water.

Natural, concave items with holes in them, such as shells, are great for water play. With a mixed age early elementary group, after observing a small stream, the children started playing poohsticks, dropping a stick or other natural item into the stream and follow it as long as they could. They eventually considered how they might transport more items at once or things that didn't float. Carla was able to pull out the recyclables, tape, tools, and other materials, and the children started creating their own vessels to transport materials downstream.

Many museums and some outdoor play spaces have opportunities to interact with water with an engineering mindset. Durable water tables with multiple levels and troughs, such as the Nature to Play Water Trough System from Rusty Keeler, move water from one place to another and allow children to experiment with water flow and interact with water up close. Various funnels, tubes, and recyclables attached to a chain link fence also allow for water flow exploration. Plus, it's a great way to cool off on a hot day!

Tools for Water Play:

- Gutters
- PVC pipe sets
- Foil formed into a shallow "river" or boat
- Clear tubing
- Drainage pipes (with or without holes)
- Funnels
- Connector tools, such as twine, chenille stems, heavy-duty gear twist ties)
- Plastic recyclables
- Colanders, pitchers, or pouring devices in a variety of sizes
- Stainless steel bowls and buckets
- Dishpan tubs
- Spray bottles
- Squirt bottles
- Floating solar water fountains

Books on Water Play

Lindstrom, Carole. 2020. *We Are Water Protectors.* New York: Roaring Brook Press.

Lindstrom, Carole. 2023. *Autumn Peltier, Water Warrior.* New York: Roaring Brook Press.

Sanchez, Anita. 2022. *Hello, Puddle!* New York: Clarion Books.

Megan Gessler recounts how the children in her care started putting things down the storm drain, as children are prone to do when there is a seemingly empty hole. While she had tried the "stop it" approach (telling them to stop it and hoping they would), she ultimately took a different approach. She brought in a long, black, accordion-style drainage tube. She collected boxes and bungee cords and provided lots of ice cubes. Children created elevation with the boxes and dumped the ice down the tube into the drain. Flashlights helped them peer inside the tube and drain to investigate what was happening.

The children explored this concept for several weeks and eventually wanted to find all the storm drains at the 1700-acre arboretum. The director of facilities provided a map of drains nearby. The children started using the map to find the drains, practicing prereading skills as they visited each of them. With subsequent rains, the water started gushing in all the streams, ditches, and even the storm drains. The children chose to follow the water flow, learning with nature and noticing the changes. As luck would have it, they found an area where water flowed under the road; trapped logs were jamming up the flow of water.

Megan said, "I wonder what will happen if more of those logs flow downstream and get stuck there." The children responded, "They will block the water!" Next, Megan said, "I wonder what will happen if they block the water." The children predicted, "It will flood the roads and then we can't get to school!" The children thought out loud, deciding to move the logs out of the water so the water flow could continue as needed. Later that day at pick up, younger siblings were putting sticks and leaves in the storm drain and the students quickly told them, "No, don't do that! It will plug up the water and then we won't be able to make it to school."

Megan reflected on the day's events. She mused that the students had that connection with and love for the water and drains and were able to take things a step further to action. The children felt powerful and like their voices mattered. They were able to speak out for nature and asked for rakes to keep the drains clear for the rest of the school year.

Living Math

Math is a way of thinking. We see it not just in numbers but also in relationships and representations. *Mathematizing* is looking for math in everyday activities. When children see that relationships and numbers are everywhere, they will be better prepared to make connections throughout life. We can build pro-math attitudes through our shared thoughts, values, and behavior. We can point out the math relationships in children's constructions with living loose parts. And we can model descriptive language for comparisons such as bigger and smaller, crunchy and smooth, and heavier and lighter.

Consider the mathematical principles surrounding us in nature every day. By just looking at leaves and flowers, we see shapes, color, form, repeating patterns, and groupings of numbers. Pause for a mathematizing walk outside. What opportunities do you have for math and natural connections where you are right now? You might have a redbud tree with heart-shaped leaves, or seed pods to measure and seeds within the pods to count. You might find sunflower heads showing Fibonacci's sequence in the growing pattern of their floret spirals,

as well as seeds and petals to count. (Count the florets from the center of the flower face to the edge, and you will likely find the number to be one from the Fibonacci sequence, often 34, 55, or 89.) The spirals of the snail and acorn caps invite mathematical observation. With a few simple tools, plus the abundance of nature and loose parts, children explore living math in ordinary play.

The Fibonacci sequence is an unending number series where each number is the sum of the two numbers that come before it. For example: 0 + 1 = 1, 1 + 1 = 2, 1 + 2 = 3, and 2 + 3 = 5.

Use what you have naturally. If you need more examples, feel free to bring in additional natural loose parts by planting interesting plants and gathering other resources. A few natural loose parts can provide opportunities for lots of math exploration.

Potential concepts to explore:

- Patterning
- Building shapes (including 3-D) with sticks
- Estimating measurements
- Sequencing the size
- Sorting and categorizing by attributes
- Symmetry

In addition to looking for natural materials to teach math, you can also bring classroom math tools outside. Too often, our mathematical tools stay in a cupboard in the classroom until we use them for a particular lesson. However, having materials available regularly gives children an opportunity to explore and experiment with the materials in a playful context. Here are a few to consider:

Scales and balances: While it's fine to bring our premade class tools outside, we can also create our own math tools as well with a log or plank over a perpendicular smaller log to create a simple balance. A hanger hung over a tree branch or fence post with attached buckets can be a simple scale.

Mirrored "books": Use two or three (or more!) large acrylic mirrors to create a "book." Carla uses painter's tape to join the seams together, with one placed on the bottom. Beyond using nature in the book to explore patterns and symmetry, there is a bonus of seeing the nearby reflection of nature in the mirrors.

Arrays: An array is any type of container, board, or recycled item that has compartments for materials to present them in a mathematical way. For example, a one-by-four array may have one row with four spots for putting things in it. Egg cartons, ice cube trays, ten frames, and hundred boards are all good arrays. Arrays can be used for sorting, one-to-one correspondence, and so much more as children build skills with living loose parts.

Potential mathematical tools and materials for outside:

Tools:

- Magnifying glasses
- Tongs
- Tweezer
- Mirrors
- Mirror "books"
- Tool apron
- Markers
- Variety of tape (electric, tree tagging, painters, masking, washi, and so on)
- Trundle wheel
- Balance
- Scale

Numbers:

- Wooden number puzzles
- Sum blocks
- Numbered rocks
- Numbered tree cookies
- Numbered footsteps
- Numbered tiles
- Numbered calendar
- Shapes
- Dominoes
- Perpetual calendar pieces
- Wooden number shapes
- Blank calendars
- Date books
- Rummikub tiles
- Dice inside dice
- Wooden lawn dice
- Hundreds chart

Mark-making:

- Individual chalkboards
- Individual whiteboards
- Clipboards
- Writing utensils
- Paper
- Blank hundreds charts
- Graph paper
- Tally sheets
- Blank graph chart
- Graph paper

Containers:

- Numbered baskets
- Divided baskets
- Wooden trays
- Lunch trays
- Stainless steel bowls
- Cookie sheet with lip
- Recycled containers (such as individual applesauce or mandarin oranges)

General:

- Craft sticks
- Chenille stems
- Apple sauce lids
- Milk and other lids
- Paper plates
- Rope
- Twine
- String
- Stick-lets
- Golf tees
- Ribbons
- Pompoms of various sizes
- Sticks

Measuring:

- Tape measures
- Rulers
- Measuring cups
- Measuring spoons

Arrays:

- Egg cartons (2 by 5, 2 by 6, 5 by 5)
- Wooden garden trellis
- Ice cube trays
- Muffin tins
- Recyclables
- Ten frame
- Number chart
- Sammy the yard/meter snake
- Stick sets in unit sizes

Games and toys:

- Game boards
- Game pieces
- Timers
- Fake money
- Unit blocks
- Keva planks/Kapla blocks
- Magna-tiles

Math manipulatives:

- Unifix cubes
- Counters
- Base 10 blocks
- Fraction options

MEASURING WITH LIVING LOOSE PARTS

When exploring worms, Carla offers rulers for children to use in measuring the different lengths of the worms. They often note how the worms change sizes by stretching out or scrunching up. Rulers, tape measures, and other tools measure flowers inside the classroom as well. Other times, the flower head becomes the standard unit of measurement.

Puddle Math

Anita Sanchez, author of *Hello, Puddle!*, offers an educators' guide (https://anitasanchez.com/hello-puddle/hello-puddle-educators-guide/) of puddle- and math-related activities. She suggests, for example, using a ruler to measure the depth of a puddle and investigating for deeper spots, and using a piece of string or tape measure to find the widest spot. These can be recorded over time to look for changes. Check on the puddle regularly.

Touchy-Feely Bags

Provide a variety of fabric bags large enough for a natural item to be inside—bonus if the item is related to a plant or animal. Invite the children to explore each bag using their hands and to describe the properties of shapes, forms, and objects they find. Focus on describing what is felt rather than naming it right away. Children can also put items in the bags for others to explore. Alternatively, make a feely or mystery box by cutting an opening on the side large enough to put a hand in to feel the object inside. Items for the touchy-feely bags may include an antler, a horn, a dried shelf mushroom, a stick, a special rock, a feather, or another natural object.

Venn Diagrams and Likert Scales

Easily make a large Venn diagram by overlapping two large, plastic hoops or strings put in circles. The Venn diagram can be used in many ways. For one class, children brought in their own favorite stuffed animals and used them throughout the day as part of play and learning. During outdoor education time, we built on the concepts of *tame* and *wild* and sorted the stuffed animals into these two categories. We discussed how some cats might be feral, and we talked about how ducks might live in the wild or on farms. As interesting animals came up, children suggested adding a new hoop for other categories, such as imaginary or extinct.

The same hoops later became part of a Likert scale to understand how preschoolers and educators felt about different types of animals. Using loose parts to make smiley, straight, and frowny faces (we also talked about other feelings), participants could choose their overall feelings about a certain animal. The children could move, use expressions on their faces, and discuss how they felt about certain animals, sometimes changing their minds after the discussion.

Tallies and Graphing

Providing documentation materials and forms allows children to keep tallies of animals seen, the number of different colors of birds in their space, their favorite flowers, or their likes/dislikes after tasting a wild edible. Introduce and model ways of exploring tallies and graphing while also giving support as children find ways to research, record, and share results from their own living loose parts investigations.

Problem Solving

In all our mathematical connections, children are ultimately problem solvers, which is also a key concept of loose parts. Nicholson (1971) explained in his theory that loose parts and learning should help solve real-life problems pertinent to the children. Additionally, in

Messy Maths by Juliet Robertson (2017), she shares four questions of data analysis that are a perfect way to support inquiry and emergent learning with living loose parts. As educators, we can support students as they start wondering about something.

1. What do you want to know?
2. How can you find out?
3. What tools will help you collect the data?
4. How will you use the information?

Books for Math and Living Loose Parts

Campbell, Sarah C. 2022. *Growing Patterns: Fibonacci Numbers in Nature*. New York: Astra Books for Young Readers.

Flatt, Lizann. 2017. *Counting on Fall*. Toronto, ON: Owlkids Books.

Flatt, Lizann. 2018. *Shaping up Summer*. Toronto, ON: Owlkids Books.

Flatt, Lizann. 2018. *Sizing up Winter*. Toronto, ON: Owlkids Books.

Flatt, Lizann. 2018. *Sorting through Spring*. Toronto, ON: Owlkids Books.

Hesselberth, Joyce. 2020. *Pitter Pattern*. New York: Greenwillow Books.

Jenkins, Steve. 2017. *Just a Second*. New York: Clarion Books.

Kroll, Virginia. 2005. *Equal Shmequal*. Watertown, MA: Charlesbridge.

Kyung, Hyewon. 2018. *Bigger Than You*. New York: Greenwillow Books.

Pecaski McLennan, Deanna. 2019. *Winter Math Walk: Finding Math in Nature*. Ontario: Pecaski McLennan.

Sidman, Joyce. 2018. *Swirl by Swirl: Spirals in Nature*. New York: Clarion Books.

Slevin, Gabrielle. 2007. *Looking for Symmetry*. San Antonio, TX: National Geographic School Publishing.

Seasonal Considerations

The regular changes in the seasons allow for different opportunities. Consider these seasonal living loose parts investigations:

- Hosting a caterpillar
- Celebrating Squirrel Appreciation Day
- Hatching eggs in the classroom
- Spring and fall migration
- Animals in winter
- Animal babies
- Tadpoles and frogs

Seasons are naturally cyclical, so try to catch the rhythm of what is around you. One way Carla encourages family engagement is by asking children and their families to investigate their neighborhood. She sends home autumn treasure bags and asks families to fill them with autumn loose parts for the children to explore. She puts a note on each paper bag, with a request for a fall family walk, tips for responsible collecting, and the return date. As children bring the bags back to school, Carla spreads out light-colored ground coverings to help them see the items better.

She reads parts of the book *What's in Your Pocket? Collecting Nature's Treasures* by Heather L. Montgomery, which explores how children in the past collected items and later became scientists and invites children to responsibly create their own pocket collections. Children share, sort, and categorize collected items in smaller groups. They investigate textures, colors, smells, and curious features. Then, the children have a large bin of natural, seasonally appropriate loose parts to investigate. Carla often reads *Leaf Man* by Lois Elhert and encourages children to make their own leaf creatures with the seasonal loose parts.

Another fall favorite is "borrowing" beans to shell and having the children help with the process. Carla also buys dried dent corn to take off the cob and opens up several gourds and pumpkins for investigations. Providing tools and allowing open exploration of the materials gives children an opportunity to get to know the fall harvest more, use their imaginations, and converse over the similarities and differences of the loose parts.

> As a nature-based educator, I believe in learning in harmony with the rhythm of nature. So if it's fall, children go on nature walks to collect leaves, pinecones, acorns, and special sticks to bring back to our indoor and outdoor classrooms. My favorite tool for children is a magnifying glass because it unlocks an unseen world. As the seasons change, our access to natural loose parts changes. In winter, when much of our world is covered in snow here in northern Vermont, our loose parts activities become catching snowflakes, scooping snow, climbing snowbanks, and exploring icicles. As we shift our view to noticing the natural world, we begin to realize the play potential of what looks like a barren space.
>
> —April Zajko

In a study conducted in a nature preschool, Laura gave the children iPads to use to take photos on their daily walks through the zoo grounds and botanical gardens. Later, when we went through the photos together and talked about the images they took, we noticed most of the pictures were of their friends. But a surprising number were of animal droppings. It does make sense. At three and four years old, bathroom needs are still the focus of many conversations: "Do you need to go? Are you sure?" And animal poop is pretty interesting, as well as being right there on the ground nearer their eye level. It was notable that the children were just as interested in random bugs as they were in the more exotic elephants and rhinos. They found that the dirt and weeds growing in the sidewalk cracks captured as much attention as the formal gardens. Everything is new to them. Opportunities for teaching are everywhere! They were also quite comfortable with the technology. One three-year-old, noticing a waterfall said, "Oh. I better switch to video." He was putting together a complex series of planning thoughts on the fly: "What am I seeing? How can I best record my ideas now to share them later?"

STEM and nature go hand in hand. As children explore living loose parts, notice them regularly using math, engineering, and science principles in their play and learning.

CHAPTER 9

Getting Dramatic with Living Loose Parts

Overheard at the blackberry patch one hot and misty June morning:

> **OLDER CHILD** (calling out from a few rows away): My bucket is full, Mommy, but I'm still going to pick a few more.
>
> **YOUNGER CHILD** (nearby): MY bucket is fully almost fully full!
>
> **OLDER CHILD** (running up to the younger one): Let's compare!
>
> **YOUNGEST CHILD** (calling from behind some bushes at the end of the row): I found mud!
>
> **PARENT** (several rows away): There's a lot of berries left on the vines over here.

Even though these three children and adults seem to have different agendas—ranging from finding mud to picking more berries than one's sister to just getting the berry buckets filled and getting on with the day—time spent at pick-your-own farms, gardens, and in parks can allow children the freedom to safely explore at a distance from adults. They notice details about the plants, dirt, butterflies, and sky, and make comparisons using their senses—which berries taste sweeter? How do you know which ones will taste sour? How can you predict the difference? What are the clues? How much pressure do you need to exert with your fingertips to pull the berry off the vine without squishing the juice all over your hand? Perhaps most valuable of all are

the opportunities to be playful with language: What exactly does "fully almost fully full" mean? How does it compare to a full bucket? When we talk with children, we're not just telling them things; we are encouraging their active participation using language. The words we choose help them consider concepts in new ways. Like butterflies on blackberries, language flutters to life.

The Stories That Shape Us

Storytelling is as old as language itself. As an ancient means of providing entertainment, making connections, and passing down lessons, stories define groups of people across history. Loose parts are natural storytelling props. As soon as children start to play, they create running narratives: "You be the momma mouse over in that corner, I'll be the old granny coming into the kitchen!" Living loose parts themselves inspire stories and help children expand their stories. Watch a child messing about with rocks, sticks, or bugs. You'll soon hear the child create names for the objects, and, if you're lucky, you'll begin to see adventures unfolding.

Storytelling also helps build a sense of community with the families we serve. Greeting a parent at pick-up time with "Let me tell you about what happened today . . ." gets their attention and plants the seed for a shared bond. Families want to hear more. We get to know each other through stories. Just as molecules are built from atoms, our personalities are built from the stories we live and the stories we tell.

"Listen, and you will realize we are made not of cells or atoms. We are made of stories."

–Mia Couto, **Mozambiquan author**

Stories can spring from our memories, shared experiences, or imaginations. A good story just needs some characters in a place with a problem to solve. Children's books are a great place to start with storytelling. Once you are comfortable reading stories with character voices and dramatic pauses, practice putting down the book and asking children to predict what comes next. Then, ask them what they would do if they were in the story. Use puppets, small world props, and flannel board pieces to retell stories. Ask children to recall what happened, then ask them to propose new beginnings, middles, and endings to the story arc.

Books that Encourage Living Loose Parts Play

Archer, Micha. 2021. *Wonder Walkers*. New York: Nancy Paulsen Books.

Davis, Katie. 2001. *Who Hops?* New York: Clarion.

Ehlert, Lois. 2005. *Leaf Man*. New York: Harcourt.

Goade, Michaela. 2022. *Berry Song*. New York: Little, Brown Books for Young Readers.

Hutchins, Hazel. 2008. *Mattland*. Toronto, ON: Annick Press.

Hutts Aston, Dianna. 2011. *Dream Something Big: The Story of the Watts Towers*. New York: Dial Books.

Jenkins, Emily. 2022. *Toys Meet Snow*. New York: Dragonfly Books.

Judge, Lita. 2021. *The Wisdom of Trees: How Trees Work Together to Form a Natural Kingdom*. New York: Roaring Brook Press.

Lionni, Leo. 1993. *Let's Make Rabbits*. New York: Dragonfly Books.

Lonzano, Christin. 2015. *Island Toes*. Honolulu, HI: Bess Press.

McLerran, Alice. 2004. *Roxaboxen*. New York: HarperCollins.

Ring, Susan. 1999. *Design It! Build It!* Marlborough, MA: Sundance Newbridge.

Underwood, Deborah. 2020. *Outside In*. New York: Clarion.

Notice What You Notice

Our role as teachers is not to do the work for children, even when that might feel more efficient. Our job is to help them construct the skills they will need to learn today and throughout their lives. Young children will continue to build on the foundations we help them create long after they've left us behind. Learning is messy. The learning curve can look more like a cooked spaghetti noodle than a straight trajectory. When spending time in the company of children, engage them in real conversation. Invite children to notice and to observe. When we take a group of children outdoors, it's tempting to let our own voices dominate—pointing out each plant and providing the name for every bird we hear. Teaching these facts is important, but so is modeling quiet calm, especially for children who experience lots of chaotic activity elsewhere in life. We can teach children to simply be still and notice nature.

> Every rock or dandelion given to me on the playground became a golden opportunity to engage in a genuine conversation with a child while their brains were primed with self-selected, natural curiosity. While Mr. Wordsworth's poem around letting nature be our teacher expresses that written words could be dull, our brains are evolved to observe our world and to support spoken language. That conversation could be connected to counting, drawing, writing, and reading if valued and cultivated by an informed and caring individual.
>
> These were introduced in large group and set up as play invitations in centers. The children's writing and art about our studies were displayed around the room. Through every experience, they were speaking and listening, reenacting their experiences with puppets or props of the living things. They were isolating and segmenting the name of the creature they were writing about. They read their books to each other and proudly took them home to share them with their families. They counted, graphed, and analyzed everything. They created patterns and sequenced life cycles through movement and dance. They learned new vocabulary, sometimes in two languages, as we read engaging books and talked about experiences with each other. The curiosity in the living loose parts sparked the conversation. That conversation guided the instructional choice and was integrated into the standards-based lessons. It playfully guided practice and helped solidify each individual's learning or meaning at the level they were ready for.
>
> —Cherry Mays

Use nature walks to build language skills and storytelling opportunities. For example, take a silent walk. Afterward, gather around and talk about what each person noticed. When children are curious about what something is called, provide the name or search for it together in books or using apps. Provide opportunities for children to build language fluency by speaking and listening to each other. Use talking sticks to help children take turns talking and listening in small groups. Develop math and science understanding by pointing out relationships, comparisons, and attributes as you walk. After the walk, offer art materials as an invitation for children to represent their ideas. Make books together or fill notebooks over time with observations from walks. Revisit previous walks through their digital photos, art, and journals when planning your next walk together.

WHO ARE WE?

"Culture guides how we process information. Cultures with a strong oral tradition rely heavily on the brain's memory and social engagement systems to process new learning. Learning will be more effective if processed using the common cultural learning aids—stories, music, and repetition" (Hammond, 2014).

Learning new vocabulary and words in more than one language helps children think about even more ideas and the connections between them. Having conversations with experts exposes children to new knowledge, but also new ways of expressing ideas. Guest speakers could include experts that you might bring in to talk with children about living loose parts. Gardeners or greenhouse employees, school groundskeepers, family members with pets, zookeepers, docents from zoos and aquariums, park rangers, or pet-store and animal-shelter employees. Other ways to spark children's thinking and spur conversations that build language fluency, or provocations, could include the following ideas.

Share live webcams or video clips of wild animals moving in their habitat. Encourage children to move like the animals and talk about what the animals are doing and predict what they may do next. Nest cams are also great options.

Assist children in making stop-motion videos with photos of their living loose parts, revisiting the photos with children to talk about what they did, and ordering the photos to retell their story of learning together.

Provide miniature plants and animals, barns, houses, peg dolls or little people, as well as pebbles, tree cookies, and grass or sand for small world play, allowing children to act out storylines and retell favorite books with the mini materials.

Story walks connect children's picture books with nature walks, connecting literacy and nature inspired by StoryWalk. Many parks and communities have created displays along a path holding pages of the book in each display. By following the path, visitors can read the whole book. While many have created DIY approaches laminating book pages, printing them on banner fabric, and/or sticking them on moveable signs, this concept was created by Ann Ferguson and developed with Rachel Senechal. This concept can even be applied to the outdoor classroom, with a makeshift path to follow a story in the outdoors. This allows for active movement—not asking children to sit still during a story, being immersed in the great outdoors, and exposure to living loose parts. Find out more about this approach, logistics, and pricing at https://33dad4b7-7401-4dae-b26d-cbd0aa5ca53c.filesusr.com/ugd/0f622b_e1b3745b5e75441fa50ba88274da79fb.pdf.

Rather than passively listening to a story on the group time rug, the story is broken up into chunks that require movement between pages. If the book is about animals, this is a perfect time to use our bodies like the animals as we slither, fly, or crawl from one page to another.

Telling Our Own Story

Why should we tell our own stories? A storyteller from Los Angeles once shared that he had been wracking his brain to come up with a new original story for preschoolers when he noticed a couple of birds in the parking lot. When he entered the classroom, he still hadn't invented a story to share, so he just said, "I was really trying to think of a new story for you when I saw two birds outside." The children began to excitedly talk over one another, "One time, I saw two birds!" "I saw two birds, too!" The lesson here is that stories need not be elaborate or even fully formed to get children excited about them. We can work together with children to tell the stories of our shared experiences and learning journeys.

Stories can be shared in dramatic retellings for an audience, written into class-made books, recorded in podcasts, illustrated on posters or documentation boards with photos and drawings, and included in news articles and grant reports. Even babies and toddlers will join in the retelling of their favorite stories with excited babbling, pointing, and singing repeated phrases.

In Hawai'i, the term *talk-story* refers to chatting with friends or remembering old times. Laura's parents' families in the Ozarks have a similar tradition of "going visiting." Perhaps you have a precellphone-era tradition in your family. Sharing informal conversations that paint small portraits of our past can help us form lasting bonds with our students, their families, and our co-workers. Stories help us frame our experiences as positive or funny, even when they were awful in the moment. When everyone shares personal stories, together we can fill in missing voices that may not have been honored in the past. We can seek out authentic books by Native authors and marginalized people whose stories add to the whole of the human experience. The stories we share should be respectful of everyone and avoid making groups of people seem strange or exotic. Stories can celebrate our strengths, whether the teller is young or old, frail or fit, typical or divergent—and help us see that we are more alike than different in our human family.

> It started with the children. They are such social beings and interested in each other. My instruction, both direct and guided, involved the children moving, talking, counting, and comparing themselves. We used our bodies to make the letter shapes of our names. We sorted and compared what color shoes we wore. We made patterns with our sounds and the lengths of our hair, all the while talking and listening. For independent practice, we built models with found objects, which led to drawing, writing, and reading to each other. We then began a collection of things that children had found, which they could use as needed. I brought in natural objects

such as nests, shells, seeds, and the occasional dead insect for exploration. These experiences helped them recall and apply the content taught because it was connected to them as individuals and their friends.

—Cherry Mays

COMFORTABLE CHILDREN ARE MORE COMMUNICATIVE

In our search to better understand all children, especially speakers of languages other than English and nonverbal or preverbal children, we need lots of tools in our toolbox. Each child is different. Effective tools might include posted signs with diagrams, gestures, sign language, pictures, core boards, and other assistive technologies for communication. Even puppets can be less threatening for some children to talk to than other children or adults. Some young children, especially those who have limited group experiences, may find everything about a classroom overwhelming. It is helpful to arrange a large classroom into cozier areas on a child-sized scale.

Children on the autism spectrum may have specific sensory needs. They might be more comfortable with less visual clutter in the room, lower lights, or even just being outdoors. Programs have found that providing an option to do center work indoors or outside allows children more control to work calmly and stay focused.

I [Laura] have found a few children over the years who have difficulty communicating directly with me are more comfortable talking to a puppet at first. I knew a child a few years ago who would only talk through his two favorite animal puppets for much of his pre-K school year. However, by the end of the year, he was able to talk directly to his teacher and classmates. He went from saying just one word in the fall (*mama*) to saying hundreds of words by spring. Puppets can be as simple as an old tube sock with sewn-on eyes or elaborate and lifelike. They can be used by a teacher for group lessons and by children when leading lessons or when playing in centers. Puppets can even come outdoors to lead a walk or add another language experience to outside play.

DRAMATIC PLAY

Dramatic or pretend play happens when children role-play real-world activities like actors on stage, with or without props. Dramatic play allows children to explore other people's actions, thoughts, and feelings. It lets them go through the actions associated with various careers and hobbies, such as working as a chef or being a veterinarian, dancer, or hiker. We often notice children replaying their observations of family and friends as they practice verbal skills.

Whether in a designated center of the classroom, outdoors, or any other setting, dramatic play includes learning specific vocabulary related to play themes, exploring different types of social interactions, and practicing the social give-and-take of coordinating roles with other players. Dramatic play allows children to practice self-regulation, which is especially important for children who have limited opportunities to play with other children outside your program. Emotions often dictate a child's actions, but they must organize their ideas and desires and find the right words to play effectively with others. Dramatic play teaches conflict resolution by giving children

opportunities to see others' points of view and generate solutions together when conflicts arise. It empowers children to become anything they want—from a mother lion to an airplane. It allows children to control the outcome and truly choose their own adventures.

Play also can be therapeutic for children who've experienced trauma. According to the Centers for Disease Control and Prevention (2023), almost two-thirds of participants in the multidecade (and counting) Adverse Childhood Experiences study experienced adverse events during childhood. As teachers, we can build protective factors to offset negative events. Lessons learned during Laura's master's degree practicum in a play therapy office translated directly to her urban pre-K classroom at that time and across the years since then. Providing opportunities for drawing or painting on blank paper allows children an outlet to express their ideas and process their thoughts. Sensory experiences such as working with natural clay and scooping and pouring sand or water are calming. Replaying observations with loose parts allows children to make sense of their experiences.

Structured and Unstructured Dramatic Play

In structured dramatic play, an adult puts out props that dictate certain expectations for the play. Setting up a restaurant center with a checkered tablecloth, plates, a serving tray, and menus will often lead to children acting out roles of diners and waiters. Unstructured dramatic play allows children to choose from a variety of props to live out their own ideas and experiences. Both types of dramatic play help children build vocabulary and develop understanding. It is also possible to combine these two types as children may use props in new ways or plan together with their teachers for innovative play concepts.

The Teacher's Role in Dramatic Play

Our first job is to create a safe environment. This includes removing choking hazards and assessing and mitigating the risk of sharp edges or corners. Dramatic play props provide an opportunity to reflect the diversity in the group and in the world. The books, photos, and props we use can allow children to explore cultures, physical abilities, ages, gender roles, and ethnicities. We can support this play by providing everyday clothing, dishes, and utensils from a variety of traditions. We can play background music and teach songs from different cultures.

the joy of learn

We can introduce cooking tools that children might not encounter otherwise, such as tortilla presses, bamboo steamers, and barbecue grills. Teachers can support and extend the play without taking over.

Observations during dramatic play can be used for reflection in large-group meetings and planning future play experiences with the children. Our most important role as teachers is to help children with less-developed social skills enter the play and to provide opportunities to practice those skills. Everyone deserves to feel included. Living loose parts in dramatic play can include seeds such as dried corn on the cob, real or reproduction animal pelts, puppets, realistic plastic animals, and props to support role-play.

Prop Boxes

Incorporate individual children's interests when creating prop boxes with loose parts. Reach out to families and friends for donations, once you have a wish list. Think of creative storage solutions so you can rotate items and store those not in use. Consider exchanging popular prop boxes with other teachers. Include a contents list inside each box. Assign a volunteer to clean and inspect the props regularly for missing or broken pieces.

Living loose parts inspire creative use of language and role play. This play can be supported by adding props appropriate for your group of children. When gathering and curating loose parts collections, consider the ages of the children that your program serves. What do you know about their patterns of play? How can you accommodate their favorite activities in dramatic play with loose parts in ways that are safe and inviting for each age group and developmental level? The following chart may help you think about these considerations.

Living Loose Parts Dramatic-Play Inspirations by Age

12–24 MONTHS	24–36 MONTHS	3–4 YEARS	5+ YEARS
Materials to explore using five senses: herbs, fruits, and vegetables	Bags and baskets to fill and empty and transport loose parts	Containers to collect and sort loose parts: acorns, rocks, leaves, assorted seeds and sorting trays	Farmers market props for classifying and role play
Nature items and pots, bowls, and spoons or sticks for stirring	Capes and simple animal costumes for role play, scarves	Puppets and toy animals to create stories and build habitats Camping and campfire props	A stage for re-creating storylines Costumes and props that reflect stories you've been reading
Shady spot outdoors, sticks and containers to bang and shake to make noise Outdoor sand table or sandbox	Sandboxes with kitchen and garden tools and watering cans	Mud kitchen, garden tools, and dirt-digging area	Magnifying glasses, balance scales, infrared thermometers to compare surface temps, windsocks, prisms

Loose parts promote innovative vocabulary and language fluency in the dramatic play and home living areas, while promoting pretend play throughout the environment. Arrange furniture to add extra space in the areas where children naturally gravitate, such as dramatic play centers. Regularly remove materials that children are beginning to lose interest in, and refresh with new ones. Incorporate math and science by adding tools for measuring and weighing natural loose parts. Promote language by taking and displaying photos of the children working, to revisit later and talk about what's happening. Dramatic play provides language-enriching practice to build social and academic skills throughout your program.

Maple Sugaring

Dramatic play happens outside as well as indoors, providing even more rich language opportunities. One large maple tree in our space became a focal point as we watched the squirrels, collected samaras (helicopter seeds), and spun and spun our bodies around like maple seeds. We hugged the tree, found a drey (squirrel's nest), and played with the leaves and sticks. Each season brought a new surprise. In late winter as days warmed above freezing and while nights were still cold, Carla introduced the concept of maple sugaring with the preschoolers. Children were able to help tap the tree, taste the sap, and then watch a demonstration (with the fire roped off and additional supervision) of boiling the sap down into syrup. In addition to smelling the fire and evaporating sap, children tasted a small spoonful of syrup, enticing all the senses!

Not only do children get to explore maple syrup through their senses, but they also have a variety of dramatic play props to reenact the experience and try out new vocabulary by playing Sugar Shack. Carla brings in small stainless steel buckets, logs, sticks, pots, small hand drills, short stumps, spiles (the tool that allows the sap to flow), grates, and other materials that allow the children to explore the concept of maple syrup. One Pokagon Band of the Potawatomi preschool class had a sugar shack set up in the classroom during sugaring season as well.

Of course, this is a seasonal natural foraging option available only in specific geographic regions. What opportunities for learning new language expressions to build fluency through dramatic play with living loose parts are specific to your area?

Animal Play

Children are naturally drawn toward animal play. They try to become like the animal, perhaps investigating how we as humans are like other animals. There are a variety of opportunities to investigate and connect with animals beyond just interacting with live ones. Examples include the following:

- Puppets (Folkmanis is a great brand that features more realistic-looking puppets)
- Costumes (and materials to make their own)
- Stuffed animals
- Wooden or plastic animal figurines (Carla likes the Incredible Creature line from Safari)

- Games (try OuiSi Nature—such beautiful pictures of animals and nature)
- Fabric animals
- Magnet sets of animals
- Puzzles
- Pattern block activities
- Edible animal crafts

While children play with these items, they often invent elaborate stories and dramatic play. Through their play, children continue to build empathy for animals, as David Sobel (1996) mentions: "Cultivating relationships with animals, both real and imagined, is one of the best ways to foster empathy during early childhood. Children want to run like deer, to slither along the ground like snakes, to be clever as a fox and quick like a bunny. There's no need for endangered species here—there are more than enough common, everyday species to fill the lives of children. And the environmentally correct notion of not anthropomorphizing animals can be thrown out the window."

One school-aged child "adopted" a toy snake during a summer loose parts session. She created a home for it and cared for it throughout the afternoon. When Carla returned the next summer for another session, the child immediately asked where the snake was. Her connection to the toy snake became real as she thought about its needs and how she might care for it. Another child in the same program used a skunk puppet to protect the den the children were making. It became a line of defense, complete with hissing, stomping, and potential spraying, just like a skunk would. Children were learning not only animal names but also the concepts and terminology related to their habitats and behaviors.

In a Tinkergarten class, children learn about dog sleds and the animals that pull them through an animal-information card, which includes guessing clues, interesting facts, a song, and movement ideas and options.

Then, children might be inspired to incorporate huskies into their play, using boxes, cookie sheets, ropes, and backpack "halters" to haul a variety of weighted items over snow or dry land. By becoming the husky, children can understand more about how these dogs are meant to run and pull and are an essential part of life up north. Find out more about this Tinkergarten DIY activity at https://tinkergarten.com/activities/push-and-pull.

Whether learning about dog sleds and maple sugaring, reenacting squirrel and bird observations, or talking about collections, living loose parts go hand in hand with language development. Components of literacy development—vocabulary, comprehension, and fluency—incorporated authentically through children's spontaneous dramatic play greatly increases opportunities to practice new skills. Children are thus better able to remember what they've learned and make connections to new concepts.

CHAPTER 10

Living Loose pARTS

The arts can be integrated into living loose parts in many ways. Children often find ways to express themselves with natural items. In this chapter, explore possibilities with the visual arts, be inspired by environmental artists, and consider dance and sound-making as part of the arts.

Visual Arts

A few years ago, Laura conducted a study with campus preschool children in collaboration with art majors. Each four-year-old child was matched with a buddy from the art class to explore using clay. Some of the college students thought, "These kids are just little. I'll need to show them what to do step-by-step." One proceeded to roll a snake with the clay. She asked her preschool buddy to "make one just like mine," and in this way proceeded to show the child how to make a clay person—arms, legs, and body. The child stayed with her for about five minutes but was soon bored and began using the seat of her art stool as a steering wheel and "driving" it around the studio.

Across the room, another art student gave his preschool buddy a glob of clay and began telling a story as they squeezed the stiff terra cotta clay to warm it up and make it pliable. Each of them added to the story and created mountains, trees, and a family of foxes with trails and dens out of the clay as their story progressed. To look at their creation, you might not recognize what it represented. But if you listened, you could see exactly what they had in mind. This particular child had a diagnosis of attention deficit disorder, but there was no evidence of it in this activity. It was just two new friends creating art together. They were deeply engaged for the entire forty-five minutes.

When we give children coloring sheets or other predrawn forms and crayons or paint, we are just asking them to add color to someone else's idea. We can't learn what they are wondering about or even see what they know. Children need open-ended materials, such as large pieces of paper, a variety of brushes, and enough time to express their own ideas.

The more adventurous among us can create art with animals. You may have seen elephants with paintbrushes or snakes leaving looping trails across a canvas, but animal art is also possible on a smaller scale. Children can take worms from muddy soil and let them wriggle across paper leaving "painted" tracks or let June bugs track through nontoxic paint on paper.

In some programs, children use their bodies as a canvas for paint or washable markers. Even a paintbrush with no paint is a sensory experience. One program suspended paper lanterns from the ceiling for children to paint while dancing to music. Other settings have attached bells to the paintbrushes to add sound to the painting options. Children might shine flashlights around the walls and ceiling to the changing tempos of music in a darkened room during rest time, or make clay impressions of their fingertips or toes. All of these ideas include our wonderful bodies and artistic expression.

Additionally, natural dyes are a great way to use materials from lunches, meals, or the destruction of other living loose parts. Many natural materials can be broken down or added to water to create natural dyes. We have done this with onion skins, beets, and other farm scraps. But many wild materials are also suitable, including many flowers, walnut fruits/husks, berries, soils, and so on. **Safety note:** It's important to keep in mind the clothing children are wearing with these activities and the toxicity and edibility of any liquids that might end up in a child's mouth.

Environmental Art

Several artists use ephemeral, land-based art to connect with nature and the local, place-based options available. The entire space becomes possibilities for artwork and exploration. Often, Carla shares examples of these artists' work as inspiration and encourages children to explore opportunities with found natural items in their vicinity to create. Here are a few resources she really likes and options for exploring these artists:

- Chelsey Bahe does great work, often highlighting nature play. Several times a week, she leaves artistic creations on stumps along the trail at a nature center in Minnesota. People now specifically watch for her new creations. She adds pictures to her Facebook page, Take 'Em Outside. She is a huge play advocate and encourages following the child's lead outdoors.
- Andy Goldsworthy's eighteen books and four documentaries record the ephemeral nature of his sculptures. His art is made with elements he finds in nature and manipulates. He uses photography to document the decay process that changes his work over time. A few sculptures are meant to be permanent, while some last only a few hours before they are reclaimed by time or tide. The documentaries detail his process and the tools he uses: "The work itself determines the nature of its making. I enjoy the freedom of just using my hands and 'found' tools—a sharp stone, the quill of a feather, thorns. I am not playing the primitive. I use my hands because this is the best way to do most of my work. If I need

tools, then I will use them. Technology, travel, and tools are part of my life and if needed should be part of my work also. A camera is used to document an excavator to move earth, snowballs are carried cross country by an articulated truck."

- In his book *Stickwork*, Patrick Dougherty chronicles many of his whimsical stick creations from across the world. Carla was able to volunteer on one build, starting on the first day collecting willow in areas to be mowed next to the road. She added more sticks and structure midway through the build and then did finishing touches, such as adding mud to exposed willow cuts. Because willow can regenerate in the ground, you often see the sculptures sprouting, making for true living loose parts sculptures. If you have ample sticks, this is a great way to get started with outdoor creations. Dougherty said, "Sticks are something we all have in common. Everybody knows sticks—the twigs and branches picked up on grandfather's farm; the branches woven in grandmother's basket. Somewhere threaded in all the public mass is a common thread, and that thread is the human spirit."

- In Marc Pouyet's book *Simple Land Art through the Seasons*, he shows the seasonal nature of land art through the photography of his creations. This inspiration seems more doable for children, and it is a great study in lines, textures, and natural elements. In *Land Art in Town*, the artist shows art and nature in whimsical spots, reminding us that nature is all around us, wherever we may be.

- James Brunt is a land artist who uses natural, place-based materials and is the author of the book *Land Art: Creating Artworks In and With the Landscape*. Circles, mandalas, and spirals dominate his often collaborative work made of sand, rocks, pinecones, leaves, and other parts of nature.

- Richard Shilling's website, Land Art for Kids, offers instructions and many examples for creating land art. Richard mentions, "Land art for me begins with seeing the world and nature through a child's eyes. I am grateful that it is something I have never lost. Making natural sculptures allows me to indulge a little longer in that child's world. Whether you are proficient or just dabbling, an adult or a child, making a sculpture or just kicking through fallen leaves, it is all the same to me. It's all about being outside experiencing all nature has to offer." Find the website at: https://www.landartforkids.com/.

- Josie Iselin's art, Heart Stones, is a collection of hearts made of stones and rocks. It is an inspiration to keep looking for art in nature, without even having to make it ourselves. Art is in nature if we will but look for it.

- Nick Neddo makes all his own art supplies from nature. An easy way is to make your own "carbon" for drawing with the sticks from the campfire. His books, *The Organic Artist* and *The Organic Artist for Kids*, show ways to use nature to create our own art supplies (adapted from Gull, 2018).

These artists show how loose parts have been part of their work. Consider sharing examples and allowing children to make their own creations. Beautiful coffee-table books can be expensive but may be available in thrift stores or public libraries. Teach children to handle books respectfully. Model how to hold and carry them and how to turn pages without tearing, using clean dry hands. Finding inspiration in others' art and then taking time to explore the creative process ourselves allows teachers and children to express ideas and share identity with each other and the artists who spark our creativity.

Some environmental artist-inspired living loose parts activities you might try:

- Create nature faces from natural loose parts such as leaves, sticks, and petals
- Make clay faces on trees with playdough or natural clay
- Frame nature using garage sale picture frames or plexiglass rectangles to define loose parts nature art
- Explore colors from natural items
- Use paint chips to find seasonal colors
- Paint with mud, using different soils and water to create a masterpiece
- Create growing patterns, such as mandalas, with natural objects
- Make artwork with snack items during snack time

What loose parts environmental art options happen in your place?

Movement and Dance

When groups of children are left to their own devices, they naturally begin to play. If they start to play hide-and-seek, that gives us a natural introduction to learning about camouflage. If they start to play chase, that's an introduction to predators and prey. Our bodies themselves are living loose parts that can help us understand other living systems.

If you have watched young children, you know their bodies are wired to move. Any aspect of nature can be explored through movement. For example, choose some appropriate music, and ask the children to think of the wind as they move. Create the life cycle of a butterfly or a rainstorm through movement, dance, and loose parts to show understanding of the concept.

DANCE AS STORYTELLING

Animals or plants can inspire movement and exploration. For example, on a card, put one or more pictures of an animal, along with some interesting facts, a related song, and the animal's movements. Start by brainstorming the various verbs the creature may carry out. For example, a squirrel sleeps, digs, jumps, runs, climbs, hides, eats, scratches, rests, and more. Invite the children to explore these movements with their own bodies.

We often find children naturally start moving like a worm, squirrel, or cat as part of their play, especially when they have had recent animal exposure. Carla made a set of cards related to different bird actions, highlighting birds native to her area. As children get into bird mode, the cards become a spark for movement and play options. Children begin to peck like an American robin, scoop like a pelican, and paddle like a wood duck. The children use movement, dramatic play, and animal perspective-taking to learn about the natural, place-based setting.

SHADOW DANCE

There are several shadow-play dance groups, such as Attraction, Pilobolus, VERBA, and Catapult, that have competed on talent shows in the last ten years, mesmerizing us and reminding us of the power of using our bodies in connection with shadow play. With a large white screen or sheet, a projected light source, their bodies, and simple props and loose parts, they create images set to music that illustrate and tell a story. While we think of this as movement, it also includes many scientific principles, making it multimodal and multidisciplinary.

In the following simple example for first-grade students from PACE Online (Acadiana Center for the Arts and Lafayette Parish School System, 2020), the educator shares how to use a scarf for nonlocomotor and locomotor shadow play (https://www.youtube.com/watch?v=yxDcfzAVGzI). Included are descriptions with variables of moving our bodies up and down with a scarf, moving around the fabric, and relationships with space. So many preposition options are reinforced as well: *above*, *around*, *over*, *behind*, *in front of*, and more. The educator suggests the following essentials for shadow dance:

- Flashlight or light source
- Scarf or piece of fabric
- Wall or screen
- Props/loose parts
- Our bodies

Beyond using our bodies, shadow puppets have long been used in China, India, Iran, and Nepal, as well as various areas of Southeast Asia, such as Indonesia, Cambodia, Malaysia, and Thailand. Shadow theater is a classic approach to entertainment and exploration, often using shadow puppets. Shadow dancing can become a part of options and play in our environment, with our bodies an integral living loose part, especially as we investigate natural processes, animals, and plants.

Paola Lopez from Kinderoo Academy shares how this was explored in her setting, with the observations written by Gabriela Urdaneta, one of the educators there.

> The human body possesses its own language, complete with a unique grammar and code of symbols for communication. Within the body lies the origin of thought formation, as it narrates emotions, experiences, and stories through a "voice" expressed in movement. Speaking without words is akin to communicating solely through gestures. These gestures play a crucial role in deciphering the meaning conveyed through bodily movements.
>
> In our classroom, movement permeates every moment. Children shift objects from one place to another, navigate the spaces within the classroom, and attentively observe the trajectory of sliding or self-propelled objects. Moreover, they attune themselves to their own bodies, instinctively responding to music by expressing themselves through a language of emotions and intentions.
>
> In response to these observations, we created an immersive experience filled with music. As the music played, the children began moving individually. Some were inspired to imitate the movements of their peers, joining the dance. The story unfolded not through words, but through the language of the body, accompanied by the enchanting power of music. The participating children, aged between one and two years, communicate daily using various languages, both verbal and nonverbal. Their body and mind concoct narratives that come alive through movement. They explore and perceive their surroundings through their senses, crafting stories that can only be expressed through the bodily narration of continuous movement, guided by the music they hear.

Amidst these tales of transformation through movement and music, a beautiful discovery emerged: the children encountered their own shadows. As they took simple steps, their shadows followed suit, projecting in different directions with each movement. Objects introduced into their dance became intertwined with the narrative told by their body language. Children never separate their actions from their thoughts. They learn through their bodies, an ongoing process that unfolds in every aspect of their lives. This became evident as I observed the children's fascination with the way their shadows moved in response to their every action.

Curiosity, logical thinking, cause and effect—these were among the concepts I witnessed during this experience. Joy radiated from the children's faces, reflecting the beauty they wove within their minds. Their interactions birthed a captivating narrative of movement, music, light, and shadow.

With older children, Jenny Gallego, a teacher at Kinderoo Academy, shared additional exploration with shadow, music, and movement.

We initiated our session with thought-provoking discussions about movement. What does movement entail? Wind, running, dancing—motion, change in position, the act of propelling oneself in any direction. We delved into when we can observe movement. Surfing, riding a roller coaster, playing on the playground, even during meals—movement manifests in various directions. Seesaws move up and down, swings sway back and forth, opening a door involves pushing and pulling, and of course, dancing.

We explored the question of what can move. Animals, people, cars, wind, clouds, the sun, the moon—everything experiences movement. Even our own bodies are constantly in motion. Nature itself is filled with waves of movement.

Next, we contemplated how to set things in motion. There are numerous ways to make objects move—through impact, blowing, pushing, and pulling. But how can we make shadows move? By moving our hands, wiggling our fingers, or simply moving in front of a light source. By manipulating the light, such as moving it back and forth, shadows come to life. When the light retreats, we observe the shadow fading away.

Movement, even in dancing, breathes life into shadows. In this proposal, after our discussions, the children engaged in play with their shadows. Shadow play and body movement became creative and expressive activities, encouraging them to explore, use their imagination, create, and discover the effects of light and shadow. Through their bodies, they crafted different shapes and movements, fostering both physical and cognitive development.

We also explored how music can influence shadow play. Music adds an extra layer of sensory stimulation and engagement to shadow play. We observed that when music combined with shadow play, it became a multisensory activity that evoked various moods and feelings depending on the type of music. The tempo and rhythm of the music influenced the speed and movement of the shadows. Upbeat and lively Latin music led to faster and more energetic shadow movements in the majority of children.

"I can't see my movements well because my shadow is faster."—Oakley

"My shadow is happy."—Zera

On the other hand, slow music elicited peaceful and calm movements, fostering a delicate atmosphere and allowing for more detailed observations.

"I can see how my shadow moves up and down."—Vicente

"I can make my shadow move in different places—close, far, up, and down."—Oakley

"I can make my shadow big, small, or even disappear."—Leo

Furthermore, the children were encouraged to incorporate materials into their shadow play. With the prompt, "How can the materials transform your movements?" children turned into frogs, butterflies (with fabric), and a rainbow bird (when she approached three colorful lights).

"The shadow changes when we dance with a friend."—Zera

"I can be a dragon using the flowers."—Vicente

Sparking movement with shadows and dance can be a wonderful way to allow children artistic freedom and expression.

Music

Making music and exploring sounds is another way to incorporate rich learning with loose parts.

PERCUSSION

Many of us enjoy the unique percussion antics of groups such as Stomp and the Blue Man Group. In these performances, percussionists use items such as brooms, water, buckets, garbage cans, street signs, wheel rims, pots and pans, sinks, matchsticks, their bodies, and so much more to make a beat. And they are so engaging—they make us want to explore sound as well. As a parent of teen percussionists, Carla often finds that her house has become a sound lab as the children explore sound with empty water bottles, metal bowls or sheets, retainer containers, the table, and the wall. Really, they explore everything for potential sound quality. While they do have some "real" instruments strewn about, bodies, dishes, and found items are often the base of sound experimentation and exploration.

Likewise, her family has been to many percussion concerts. In one number, the women entered the space with an old magazine in their hands, ripping, crumpling, tearing, clapping, and rubbing the paper. This became a main component of the piece as they moved through improvisation of interacting with various elements—paper, metal, snapping, and other explorations. Another concert allowed students to explore what they had been learning and experimenting during percussion camp. One piece had a triangle for each of the six students. The way they used the triangles was creative as they discovered how they could control the vibrations by how they held the triangle. They combined movement, throwing, and catching the triangles for different effects. Another piece included metal bowls of water, triangle beaters, and crotales (a type of cymbal). The percussionists played the cymbals together and eventually put a vibrating cymbal into the water, which changed the tone and pitch. Both composers and percussionists pushed the edges of exploring the capacities of the materials around them.

Likewise, young children can and do experiment with sound in a variety of ways. After reading the book *Max Found Two Sticks* by Brian Pinkney, Carla likes to take students on a sound exploration walk. Each child generally has access to, but is not limited to, a stick, an inexpensive spoon, and a child-sized wooden mallet. With a few parameters for safety (such as no banging on glass and staying away from the road and within supervision range), they explore sound in their space by tapping, hitting, pounding, and banging on materials around them. They compare the sounds of rocks, concrete, a bicycle stand, nearby trees (gently!), bare soil, the grass, along the fence, and so on.

Other times she sets out a sound lab. After spreading a large tarp on the ground, she puts out a variety of items. Stainless steel bowls and pails, plastic bowls with lids, sticks, metal whisks and spoons, silicone basters, a variety of small instruments, tree cookies of various thicknesses and sizes, pots and pans, lids, cookie tins, cowbells, and other odds and ends are available to explore sound in any way children may desire, often in conjunction with the environment as a whole. The children sometimes spontaneously create their own musical parade through the space.

Carla has also brought stainless steel bowls, rocks, water, and sticks to a community event with families. While these weren't combined together in the play space set up, the children began combining them. "Plop, plop, plop" as rocks dropped into the water in the bowls. "Ting!" as a stick hit the side of the bowl. "Swish" when the stick stirs around. Children experiment with the sounds as the materials interact. Nearby parents were amazed at how long children explored the materials, noting these were all easily found items they had at home.

An oscilloscope or an app such as GarageBand can make sound waves appear visible by representing the vibrations on a screen and changing with variations in volume and tempo. Children can experiment by making noises by tapping on various surfaces with a spoon or drumstick, or walking up and down steps in house shoes, heels, tap shoes, or tennis shoes, and comparing the sound waves they see.

Another book to explore sound is *A Beautiful Noise: The Music of John Cage* by Lisa Rogers. Cage's musical composition *Water Walk* explores water in various states (ice, steam, liquid) to create sound as part of the song. Additionally, he adds nails and other implements to his piano to alter the sounds. A preschool class Carla worked with took apart a piano as part of music class—experimenting with altering how sound is made through the deconstruction. Plus, they had unique loose parts after their project.

For another fun activity with visible sound, find an old stereo speaker—thrift shops or garage sales may be good sources—and cover it completely with plastic wrap. Mix cornstarch and water to make goop. Play music and watch the goop dance to the beat. For a demonstration, look up "non-Newtonian fluid on a speaker" videos on YouTube.

Be open to artistic expressions as you interact in your natural areas and settings. Give children permission to explore art outside with sound and movement. Children's bodies are wired to experiment, invent, and have fun. Try it yourself as well! We all need a little creativity and expression.

CHAPTER 11

Supporting Feelings and Friendship

The power of play and the healing aspects of nature can be great ways to support emotional needs in our settings. In this chapter, explore ways to support children in their big feelings, and find loose parts–inspired books that support social and emotional needs.

Social-Emotional Needs and the Power of Plenty

During the COVID-19 pandemic, children and adults missed out on group gatherings and social interactions. It will take time for us to rebuild these skills, so give yourself and the children a little grace. Living loose parts can be an antidote to social isolation. As children work alone or with a friend, their actions and conversations give us an entry to extend conversations and help them build friendship skills. The calming influence of nature lowers anxiety and encourages joy.

To build social skills, we need to have a few tools in our pockets. First, never assume that we know what's going on when conflict arises, even if we saw it happen. Approach slowly and remain calm. If children are fighting over an object, hold the object or put it away until the issue is resolved. Take time to hear each person's point of view, then ask them to suggest solutions. They may suggest using time to take turns or something that you hadn't even thought of. If they can agree, problem solved. If they can't, suggest a few solutions of your own, but make sure children have the power to choose and agree on one of them. Older children can write down their solutions, which also gives them a minute to collect their feelings.

Each time a conflict occurs, reflect on how it could've been prevented. Sometimes, we can avoid causing frustration by rearranging the space so popular areas become less crowded. If everyone wants to do the same thing at once, examine the other choices. They might be so easy that they are boring or so hard that they are frustrating. The most powerful thing we can do when setting up a space for learning is to find the right balance. Like a dance floor, our classrooms must accommodate the movement of bodies.

Having too much stuff out makes it impossible to navigate safely. Not enough stuff, and scarcity will cause conflict. Toddlers, especially, like to do what other children are doing, so make sure you have multiples of favorite objects. Little humans don't really understand "wait your turn" because they live in the moment. For them, it's now or never. Ask for donations. Share supplies with classrooms next door. Borrow from your friends. Collect and return sticks, acorns, pinecones, and rocks from your neighborhood or schoolyard. There is power in having plenty.

Responding to Temper Tantrums and Autistic or Sensory Meltdowns

It is important to know the difference between a sensory meltdown and a temper tantrum. To an observer, they can look a lot alike. A child may become red-faced and loud, possibly fall to the floor hitting and kicking, and may throw any object close at hand. It is upsetting for everyone, including the child. A temper tantrum is goal-directed. A child is having a fit because they want something and don't know how else to get it. A sensory meltdown happens when a child is overwhelmed by information coming in through their senses. It might be triggered by loud noises, extreme temperatures, or something else. There is always an antecedent with a meltdown, although you might not be able to identify it at first. As you get to know the children in your care and talk to their families, you will begin to pick up on their specific triggers. You can plan ahead to avoid most meltdowns.

During a meltdown or tantrum:

- Remain calm. It is harder for a child to regain control if they see us losing it.
- Next, move the child to a place where they are less likely to harm themselves or others. Sometimes, this will mean moving other children away.
- Do not try to reason with or teach behavioral lessons to a child while that child is in a meltdown or having a tantrum. They are not intellectually available for learning at that time.
- Focus on allowing the storm to pass safely. Raising your voice and moving too close can make it worse.
- When the child is recovering, offer a drink of water and reassurance that we all have big feelings sometimes.

- Help the child clean up any mess they made, or offer an ice pack or cool cloth for minor injuries.
- When they are feeling better, you can talk with them about what happened. They may not be able to tell you.
- Help them notice the sensations in their body that signal they are becoming upset. These might include feeling hot, feeling angry or frustrated, or having an impulse to throw something or to get away fast.
- Plan with them when they are calm about what they could try next time they notice these big emotions coming on.
- Teach relaxing techniques such as yoga, box breathing, counting, and grounding exercises (stopping to notice things they can hear, see, smell, touch, and taste).
- Weighted items such as a stuffed animal, vest, or lap pad may comfort some children. Establish this procedure ahead of time, when they are calm.
- An appropriate response to a tantrum is to make sure the child is safe, but ignore the fit.

A child in a sensory meltdown needs your reassurance. With a nod or a light touch, let them know that you understand and will help them calm down, that you will be there to help process their feelings when the storm has passed.

When considering social-emotional learning and living loose parts, Carla suggests the following:

- Get to know our own emotions—*Atlas of the Heart* by Brené Brown is an excellent resource.
- Recognize the inherent ability of loose parts to allow children to work out issues and meet their own needs.
- Create a specific kit or collection around social-emotional learning topics, such as emotions, faces, and so on.
- Include books around social-emotional learning in other kits, such as *I'm Done* in a beaver kit, *How Are You Peeling? Food with Moods* in an emotions kit, or *Be a Tree* in a tree kit or just on its own.
- Create a calm-down kit. Add sounds of nature, textures from the natural world, and lavender scents.
- Include lots of options for interacting with animals and dramatic play—puppets, costumes, fabrics, stuffed animals, plastic animals, and so on.
- Review resources from Tinkergarten. They have lots of videos, blogs, and other resources around social-emotional learning at https://www.tinkergarten.com/activities/skills/social-and-emotional-skills.
- Learn more about social-emotional theory: https://casel.org/fundamentals-of-sel/

Carla asked the Loose Parts Facebook group about social-emotional connections to loose parts and enjoyed the conversation. Here are a few notable excerpts:

> When I think about loose parts and the personal/emotional aspects of SEL, I think about:
>
> - agency (I can come up with my own ideas and make them happen)
> - creativity (I can make something new and interesting)
> - problem solving (this isn't what I thought would happen/This didn't work . . .)
> - flexible thinking (that didn't work out/this material gives me a new idea).
>
> —Sarae Pacetta

> Persistence, growth mindset, divergent thinking, sometimes collaboration and cooperation, sometimes communication, empathy, taking on other perspectives
>
> —Carla Gull

> Open-ended materials/loose parts invite schema explorations which all children recognize and will join in with others to expand their play, learning, and social skills . . . Observe children playing together and you will see this big time.
>
> —Deb Curtis

> Practically speaking, I've done lots of mindfulness and identity activities with loose parts inspired by stories (such as sharing a place that is special to us, activities that help us feel calm). I think the biggest benefits and connections are embedded in the philosophy, though, as long as we make that reflection explicit and intentional for students (such as by shifting perspective, developing solutions to problems, reflecting on personal strengths). Definitely needs to connect to the CASEL competencies in a visible way.
>
> —Beverley Anne

Children's books featuring living loose parts can support social and emotional development. Megan Gessler curated a list that may help children see through the eyes of another, imagine how things can change, and see themselves as capable of making changes. Carla starred books that also have good loose parts connections.

Nature and Loose Parts—Connected Social-Emotional Books

DEVELOPING KINSHIP AND EMPATHY

A Friend to Nature by Laura Knowles

Here and Now by Julia Denos

**Listen* by Gabi Snyder

Outside In by Deborah Underwood

Peace Is an Offering by Annette LeBox

Stick and Stone by Beth Ferry and Tom Lichtenheld

**Wonder Walkers* by Micha Archer

You Are Never Alone by Elin Kelsey

GROWTH MINDSET

**Ada Twist, Scientist* by Andrea Beaty

**Be a Maker* by Katie Howes

**Beautiful Oops!* by Barney Saltzberg

**Boxitects* by Kim Smith

Flight School by Lita Judge

Going Places by Peter and Paul Reynolds

I Am the Storm by Jane Yolen and Heidi E. Y. Stemple

**Jabari Tries* by Gaia Cornwall

**Made by Maxine* by Ruth Spiro

The Magical Yet by Angela DiTerlizzi

**Maybe* by Kobi Yamada

**Rosie Revere, Engineer* by Andrea Beaty

The Thing Lou Couldn't Do by Ashley Spires

Whistle for Willie by Ezra Jack Keats

You Are a Beautiful Beginning by Nina Laden

BECOMING AGENTS OF CHANGE

Change Sings: A Children's Anthem by Amanda Gorman

**The Fort* by Laura Purdew

**Iggy Peck, Architect* by Andrea Beaty

I Am Courage: A Book of Resilience by Susan Verde

I Am One: A Book of Action by Susan Verde

Lala's Words: A Story of Planting Kindness by Gracey Zhang

**The Most Magnificent Thing* by Ashley Spires

Say Something! by Peter H. Reynolds

**Seeds and Trees* by Brandon Walden

The Tree Lady: The True Story of How One Tree-Loving Woman Changed a City Forever by H. Joseph Hopkins

**What Do You Do with a Chance?* by Kobi Yamada

**What Do You Do with an Idea?* by Kobi Yamada

**What Do You Do with a Problem?* by Kobi Yamada

(Adapted from Gull, 2022b)

We honor nature as we become more familiar with it. The book *Be a Tree* by Maria Gianferrari, compares our human bodies with a tree while also making social-emotional connections. Carla uses this book on a walk around the preschool in an urban setting to get to know the local trees. She and the children move like trees, feel their skin, and then gently explore the bark on several trees, curl their toes down into the earth like the roots that anchor the trees, and consider how trees might communicate through underground mycorrhizal networks (a symbiotic relationship between fungi and roots). It's a perfect read-aloud to connect to a tree and our own emotions.

As we get to know our own emotions and spend restorative time in nature, we can also support the children in our care by giving them time and space in nature-rich, play-based settings.

Conclusion

Earlier in the text we asked how you might define living loose parts. As you've been on this journey with us and experimented with the concept on your own and with the children in your setting, has your understanding changed? How would you define living loose parts now? Being able to share a quick definition in your own words, along with a few examples of how you have applied it, can go a long way with stakeholders, including parents and community members.

My definition of living loose parts:

____

____

We are applying living loose parts in a place-based way in our setting by:

____

____

____

We can't predict where living loose parts will go from here, or even the exact outcome of any open-ended lesson, but we can predict that interest in loose parts play will continue to grow. Consider the 130,000-plus members of Carla's Loose Parts Facebook group, which seems to grow daily. Nature-based preschools are currently springing up quickly, with more states looking at licensing around these programs.

As Peter Dargatz asserts, we need to find ways for all children to benefit from these connections to nature and living loose parts. He says, "There simply isn't enough [time in nature]. For a myriad of reasons, people don't seem connected to nature the way they have been and, in my opinion, the way they should be. Offering opportunities to get EVERYONE connected to nature is crucial for our educational system and beyond."

Additionally, Dr. Claire Warden (2022) reminds us:

> The Earth is constantly changing, and those loose objects we play with outside such as sticks and stones are all on a journey alongside us as human beings. The pebble that children hold was once part of a mountain or under the sea; it was a rock, a stone, now it's a pebble, but it will become a fragment, a grain, particles and molecules, and as such, will be recombined in other biological and chemical processes. We are part of this constant journey where a human lifetime is nothing more than a speck of time and all the decisions we make need to be made with the benefit of future generations in mind.

We are reminded that we can embrace whatever living loose parts nature provides; thus, our journey never ends. As we experiment with and explore the world around us, we continue to find new applications and approaches to loose parts. These suggestions are just the start. Where will curiosity and loose parts principles take you and your young learners?

In our living loose parts journey, we've laid a foundational understanding, slowed down to notice opportunities, honored nature, considered the practical side of adventures outside, and explored death, decay, and decomposition. Additionally, we put on our creativity caps, related living loose parts to standards and assessment, connected STEM possibilities, and shared ideas with dramatic play, art, and social-emotional needs. Most likely you have reflected on your practice, implemented and/or allowed explorations, and been curious about applying living loose parts more fully in your setting. We invite you to continually be curious about the world around you and to give children a responsible framework for exploring nature as well.

We recognize that no two early childhood programs are exactly alike, but believe we can inspire each other's practice. We appreciate the unique expertise you bring as our reader and would love to hear how you are applying these concepts in your role working with children, educators, families, and communities. Reach out on social media at Loose Parts Play or @loose_parts_play. Your experience, perspective, and insight continue to improve practice for young children and their families. Thank you for the continuing work you do with living loose parts!

APPENDIX A

Program Highlights

Sara Evans, Green Garden Child Development Center, Metro Detroit, Michigan

I was raised in a family with close ties to nature exploration, and as a mother of two, I have based my homeschooling philosophy on it as well. For over a decade, I have facilitated nature-oriented outings for the local homeschool community and have led workshops at events to bring nature-based, hands-on learning to kids of all ages.

Most early childhood education spaces that strive to bring a focus on nature and loose parts likely don't have an employee fully dedicated to the concepts—let alone two! I am a nature specialist, and my colleague Kelly and I work closely on many projects.

Being in the north, we get all four seasons (sometimes more), so our focus tends to be on seasonal observations. Even in an urban setting, the changing seasons and how the changes affect the way we observe our surroundings is evident. When the mulberries cover the hill, we see birds swoop to the ground or squirrels causing more berries to drop from the branches. In winter, we see footprints and note the differences in the way the animals walk in the snow. We leave the seed heads of our pollinator-garden plants and watch the birds perch and peck, and we see how the bees collect pollen on those same plants in summer.

Heather Taylor, Outside School, Richmond, California

We're in an urban park, and because we're there three times a week throughout the school year, we come to know it intimately. The rangers will often ask us for information!

Loose parts and place-based learning are natural parts of the park.

Merry Lea Environmental Learning Center, Nature-Based Preschool, Indiana

Merry Lea is an entirely outdoor classroom. There are loose parts that we curate, and those that are found just because they are a part of the space. We do provide provocations, but all of our programs are intended to fulfill an ideal of "pervasive adaptability," so many loose parts are discovered in the moment and brought with us rather than being planned ahead.

Nature provides a generous supply of invitations! Ice, snow, walnuts, acorns, fallen tree leaves, grasses, and flowers/seed heads, water from a rain barrel and in wetlands, sand, gravel, and rocks from the gravel pit—all are used as loose parts in many different ways by our students. Our sit spot practice encourages engagement with the "living" part of living loose parts within a place-based experience. The space used for sit spots, including the loose parts within them, changes over time. Ice forms and melts, ephemeral flowers appear in the spring, leaves fall and decay, and repetitive activity such as drumming on a log will mark or wear away at loose parts. Animals moving through the space bring in and remove loose parts. Our learners will also modify sit spots as they move about with other activities in our classroom.

For the past two years, we have invited our students' families, our teachers, and our coworkers to donate their "live" Christmas trees after they have taken them down at home. Students have used the pile of trees as a mountain to climb. They have also worked in teams to move the trees to various places in our outdoor classroom. The trees have been positioned to become a bed and television, with students laying down on the bed and talking about what they were watching on the TV. Other students have dug holes and tried to position the trees upright. They then have decorated the trees with leaves, twigs, and other found objects from the classroom. Some of these objects they have decorated with colored pencils before adding them to the tree as ornaments. Other students have used scissors to trim the needles from the trees, noticing the differences in needles on different tree species. Still others have used the trees as cushions to leap onto. Trees have even become walls to a fort.

During sit spot time, teacher Marcos watched as a preschooler carefully threaded leaves one by one onto a protruding sapling stem that was about six inches high. He noticed the child choosing certain leaves, figuring out which were easily pierced and which were not, their characteristics, and so on.

After sit spot one early spring day, one of our students showed Carol something she had been creating during that ten to fifteen minutes. She had made what she called a fairy garden: an acorn cap that she filled with damp earth and then tucked in fresh green leaves and tiny flower buds.

At a weeklong day camp, one student really wanted to bake at camp. With some suggestions, she began "baking" at her sit spot by making mud pies over and over again each day. She was able to engage with the textures, scents, colors, and contents of soil in a way that she had never experienced before. She expressed a newfound interest in the natural world around her that she had not discovered prior to this experience.

Some children drum during sit spots using branches—on logs, on rocks, and on saplings with dry leaves on them (making a rustling sound).

Many students create small "homes" for things, using bark, twigs, leaves, and grasses. Sometimes, these homes are for creatures they have actually found in the classroom, such as earthworms, daddy longlegs, spiders, slugs, snails, or insects. One year, the homes were for pet dinosaurs, which were rocks about the size of grapefruits that several of the students had found in the classroom and claimed as their own.

Some students have used the claylike mud in one part of our outdoor classroom space to make a number of things, including tiny bowls and plates that they then use to serve "food" to other students. A few students have also used the clay to make swallow-like bird nests affixed to the side of a tree.

During a weeklong program, one group of participants made daily trips to the same location at a creek. In the warm weather, they used many loose parts, such as floating sticks and stacking stones, to navigate this space and shape the flow of the water.

One recurring practice for single-day trips, especially in the spring, is to use logs and fallen tree debris as loose parts to investigate. While these are sometimes used broadly for construction or imaginative play, they become especially alive when investigated closely. Many are covered in lichens, mosses, and fungi and have a variety of hardness and texture. Underneath every log is a world teeming with life that shapes the log and is shaped by it. All sorts of invertebrates shelter under the log to eat, stay moist, hunt, burrow, or avoid predators. Each of these invertebrates, alive in its own right, shapes the log, turning it into a mutable, "living" loose part. Sometimes, vertebrates such as snakes, salamanders, and frogs take shelter underneath these logs, narrowing and zooming in our sense of place to one much smaller than ourselves. Occasionally, children will even turn little invertebrates into loose parts themselves, collecting worms, roly-polies, or ants in cupped hands and hollows.

An upright stump with a hole in the center became a receptacle for water, a mechanics pit, and a truck engine.

Peter Dargatz, Kindergarten Teacher, Hamilton School District, Wisconsin

I love watching children (in both directed and undirected ways) use living loose parts and their creativity to make something new. Being a public school teacher, I often feel tethered to the requirements of the curriculum, so I like to stretch the boundaries as much as I can. One of our favorite art projects is when we use twigs, leaves, and prairie seeds to create posters to decorate the hallway outside our room. We also use living loose parts to create mouse houses as part of our wants and needs unit. This serves as a kickoff to an inspirational yearlong collaboration with our local children's hospital.

Here are some tips for public school educators in moving to more nature-based education:

- Start small.
- Change locations, not expectations.
- Make it a routine, instead of a reward.
- Roll with Mother Nature's punches.
- Be a proactive problem solver.
- Expect and embrace the unexpected.
- Bring nature inside.
- Emphasize emergent opportunities.
- Use your time wisely.
- It's all about relationships.
- Work hard. Play harder!
- Let kids be kids. (Dargatz, 2021)

Becky Gamache, Duluth Preschool, Minnesota

We use what we readily have available in our environments. I also found that once folks find out you collect loose parts, they often contribute pinecones from their yard, rocks from Lake Superior, skulls from their woods, and so on. When items were donated, we talked about the story of where they came from: "John's grandma was walking by the lake and found these sparkly rocks. She thought we'd like to have them," or "Sarah's family go deer hunting. They brought us these deer antlers. I wonder what we can use them for."

We always have water, liquid water color, and various containers available on below-zero temperature days. The children fill the containers with water and color it as they see fit. We wheel a cartful outside, then check on it every so often to watch the contents freeze. After they are all frozen (sometimes the same day if it is cold enough!), we bring them to the woods where they become buried treasure or gems or whatever the children use them for. After snowfalls, the colored ice chunks are buried and new play ideas crop up when they are found.

Angela Holmes-Krober, Curriculum Coordinator, The Child Study Center at the University of Central Oklahoma

I view living loose parts as a necessity in an early childhood setting. Children are born to investigate and explore their environment. My role as a teacher is to help establish a strong foundation for the love of nature. Children should be given opportunities to understand and develop a connection to the world around them.

Small world play inspired by a squirrel that frequently appears outside the classroom window.

An art display created from repurposed boxes and paper scraps.

An aerial photograph of campus, found in a campus storage unit as surplus—destined to be discarded—was repurposed as a mat in the construction area. Children often spot structures on the mat, then look for them on campus or notice something on a campus walk, then return to the classroom to search for it on the mat, using it as a map of campus and connecting the 2-D surface to objects in the real world.

Paola Lopez, Kinderoo Children's Academy, Exploratory Childcare, Florida

There is so much creativity oozing in these spaces! We cultivate the connection with living loose parts in several ways. The space is designed to be flexible and adaptable, with a variety of areas and materials that can be easily reconfigured to support different types of play and learning experiences. It includes natural elements, such as plants, water features, and rocks, which provide children with opportunities to engage with the living world and observe its cycles and changes. It encourages exploration and experimentation with loose parts that can be combined and manipulated in endless ways to create new and interesting structures and creations. Our program values process over product, allowing children to engage in open-ended, self-directed play that fosters creativity, curiosity, and problem-solving skills. The program provides opportunities for collaboration and social interaction, with spaces for group work and shared exploration of living loose parts. Overall, our educators cultivate the connection with living loose parts by prioritizing nature, play, and exploration, and value the unique perspectives and interests of each child.

By incorporating natural materials found in our local environment, educators create a deeper connection to the surrounding ecosystem and promote a sense of stewardship in young children. For example, using sticks, rocks, and leaves from the playground can help children develop a deeper understanding and appreciation of the natural world around them. Additionally, we incorporate living loose parts such as plants and animals into our preschool environments to provide children with opportunities to observe and learn about different life cycles, habitats, and ecosystems. For instance, we've used terrariums and aquariums in our classrooms to serve as a natural learning tool for young children to observe the growth and behavior of living things. We bring the natural world inside. A classroom that values living loose parts will typically have large windows to let in natural light and views of the outside world. It may also feature indoor plants, rocks, and other natural elements. Children are encouraged to touch, smell, and listen to the living loose parts in the classroom. The classroom is set up to promote exploration and discovery. Children are given opportunities to manipulate and experiment with the living loose parts, which helps them develop problem-solving skills and fosters their innate curiosity. Living loose parts provide children with endless possibilities for open-ended play. The materials can be used in a variety of ways and are not limited by specific rules or instructions. Overall, a classroom space that cultivates the connection with living loose parts is one that is designed to inspire wonder.

Our playground has brought us a new topic to study and analyze. For several weeks, multiple students have shown interest in digging in the dirt on the playground. Throughout this process, they have discovered how there are some places where they find dirt; in other places, they find sand. This led them to understand that what they would find depended on where they dug.

What we found during these excavations:

- Rocks
- Sticks
- Worms
- Roots

In these findings, the children could differentiate colors and sizes. For example, some of the worms were long and thick, and others were small and skinny. But with the roots, it was different. When they found some where there was "little" grass, they could easily move them.

However, when they found one that was under the ground and it was from a tree, they noticed how it was strong and firm, and they could not move it.

A tree root was found by Valeria, who asked, "What is this?" Ezra replied, "It's a root. The trees need it to hold on." At this point, different questions began to emerge:

VALERIA: What is a root?

EZRA: It's what holds up the tree.

VALERIA: Why does a tree need roots?

EZRA: For the water.

GUILLERMO: It helps him drink water and grow, so that he can help their friends.

MARIANA: It is the most important thing for the tree. What can we see in the root? [Observing it through the microscope*]

GUILLERMO: Water that helps them to eat.

*Note: Throughout the weeks, we have used analog and digital microscopes as a support to closely analyze the natural elements we have been investigating.

Lincoln is one of the students who has brought interest to the classroom, showing his excitement every morning by going out on the playground and digging in the dirt to find something new. His findings included rocks, sticks, and worms. Over the weeks, he has had the opportunity to observe them closely and re-create them by drawing and painting.

Ryan had the opportunity to explore, feel, and analyze these natural elements up close by observing them under a microscope and finding small details in them. To expand his exploration and learning, he has integrated art and mathematical concepts by painting and recreating an earthworm. He has also drawn a tree, in which he integrated some pieces of wool and used blocks to represent the roots.

With Ezra's lead, we have managed to consolidate answers about our research. He has discovered how we can find roots inside the earth and how the root is necessary for the tree to be able to sustain itself. Having the opportunity to observe it closely under the microscope, he became interested in recreating the root in different types of trees, inspired by a book. The first was a palm tree. He made sure to include roots in each one, but the roots varied in color. In each painting, he highlighted the importance of the earth.

Guillermo was motivated by his friends to dig in the dirt, showing surprise with what they have been able to find. Since the beginning of this research, he has always expressed the importance of water in the earth and in the trees. He has also talked about the communication that trees can have with each other to help each other—this has been thanks to online expert's videos that have supported this study.

In observing the soil and roots, Payton has found small pieces that she calls *rocks*, *sticks*, and *gems*. She has enjoyed analyzing and discussing with other students what they can observe. With her talent and dexterity in drawing, she initially recreated a root. She did not do it with a thin line but joined them, leaving some wide pieces. The next day, she took the same drawing pattern, but this time she stated that she was making a tree house by integrating color into her painting. On the third day, she used the same pattern. She then began to integrate people into her drawing.

Mariana's exploration and research were more focused on observing and analyzing these natural elements through the microscope. She enjoyed discovering the different characteristics of the earth, the sand, and the root. In the root, she found rocks and lines, always stating how the root is the most important thing for a tree. She painted using a book as inspiration, integrating different colors but highlighting the small lines of the root with white paint.

Megan Gessler, Morton Arboretum, Illinois

I would say our programming is less about the space than about the philosophy. I can talk about the many natural affordances of working in a 1700-acre arboretum, but not everyone has that access, and not every space looks like mine, yet every space has value. It's more about providing intentional opportunities to interact with nature or natural loose parts on a regular basis. If the program has a comprehensive understanding of the benefits of incorporating nature into children's learning experiences, the rest will follow.

Illinois experiences all four seasons. We have rain in the spring, which fills our creeks and provides copious amounts of magnificent mud. In summer, some of our rivers and creeks are drier and reveal more rocks or shells to explore. In fall, we have loads of seeds and leaves that change color. And in winter, we have beautiful snow.

Since we work at a living museum with live specimens, an arboretum, we often need to find the forgotten spaces for more in-depth play. A favorite spot is the composting area on the grounds, with its piles of dirt, rocks, and seasonally decomposing plant materials. It's great for sledding nearby in the winter as well.

> Another stellar day! We went to the newly christened Dirty Dump Playground (DDP) to check on our pumpkins. They are frozen, stinky, and a little moldy. But they are perfect for climbing on! We can't wait to watch the progress of composting pumpkins. We took our trowels and talked about what lives under the dirt: "What is alive? these pumpkins? the grass?"
>
> We explored the properties of water. "Is ice solid? snow? the puddle?"
>
> "Why is the dirt hard to dig, Miss Meg?"
>
> Some purple flowers were turning the snow pink. "What happens if I rub it on my hand? stick it in the puddle?"

One of my students found an amazing little dried root ball at the DDP shortly before Halloween. He held it up (It was about the same size as his entire upper torso.) and said, "Hey, Miss Meg! This looks like that lady with snake hair!"

I asked, "Do you mean Medusa?" (What four-year-old knows who Medusa is?)

"Yes!" he replied. "Can I take this home and have my brother invent a way to put this in a pumpkin to create a Medusa jack-o-lantern for Halloween?"

"Absolutely! Just send me a picture!"

Well, he lugged that heavy thing all the way back to the classroom, took it home, cleaned it up, and made an amazing Medusa jack-o-lantern! Unbelievable! These kids never cease to amaze me!

The arboretum often has large art exhibits in the space, such as trolls by Thomas Dambo and Human+Nature by Daniel Popper, which is delightful to explore with the children and often inspires their own creativity.

The children had deep thoughts about what the piece meant to them: "She's giving birth to nature." "Nature is inside of her and it's coming out." "We can see nature through her."

On Friday, we got to meet Daniel Popper, the artist who is responsible for creating our new exhibit. The children were so excited to meet him and ask questions. Mr. Popper was gracious enough to allow our class to be the first children inside this particular piece, and he got to see their reactions. They asked him what an artist is, how he thinks of his ideas, what they mean, what tools he uses, and how he makes his sculptures so large. Oh, and can he build a tarantula? His answers were perfectly suited for his audience, and he showed them how he used his tools on concrete to make it look like wood.

The children then sat down and watched the work while they made their own sculptures that they will paint next week. We also acted out sculptures with our bodies. The children would call out different things that they imagined being sculpted, and everyone would make that pose.

We hiked around the sculptures on the east side of the arboretum, watched some arborists cutting down limbs from high up in the trees, and attended our first annual Little Trees Art Show in the Sterling Morton Library. The children were beyond excited to have their art featured alongside the Nature Artists' Guild. They were so full of pride to be "real artists."

NOW IT'S YOUR TURN!

Of course, your space looks different from Megan's and other program profiles; however, what might be your takeaways? How can you incorporate art into your space? Could you invite a local artist in, or go on a field trip to explore art in nature? Would your compost heap or a pile of dirt be a prized play space for your children? Every space has value. Find the unique aspects and opportunities of yours!

As we reached out to practitioners to describe how living loose parts were part of their programs, we asked specific questions. Now, we ask those same questions to you. For our last program spotlight, your program is the focus.

- How do you notice living loose parts in your space and work with children?
- What loose parts support the play, learning, and connection to the natural world in your space?
- Can you share an experience or two to share with a focus on living loose parts?
- How are living loose parts place-based in your setting?
- What is unique about your space that cultivates the connection with living loose parts?
- What tips do you have for others exploring living loose parts?

This is not the end! This is just the beginning of your living loose parts journey. None of the highlighted programs look the same, nor do your programs. Feel free to answer these questions and combine them with pictures of living loose parts in your setting, then share on social media with the hashtag #livinglooseparts.

APPENDIX B

List of Living Loose Parts (Not Exhaustive!)

Tools

- Magnifying glasses
- Binoculars
- Loupes
- Bungees
- Tarps
- Scoopers
- Trowels
- Buckets
- Metal pails
- Tweezers
- Clamps
- Twist ties
- Muffin tins
- Bowls
- Measuring spoons
- Hammers
- Screwdrivers
- Nails
- Fabric
- Documenting tools
- Clipboards and paper
- Measuring tools
- Mirrors
- Wooden baskets
- Peelers
- Graters
- Files
- Scissors
- String
- Flashlights
- Bug jars
- Magnetic wands
- Balancing scales
- Sorting trays
- Nature research tools
- Nature word cards
- Nature viewing boxes
- Knives
- Multi-tool
- Dissecting kit
- Clay tools
- Nature journals
- Rope
- Dice
- Metal rulers

Plants

Leaves

Pinecones

Acorns

Sticks

Logs

Branches

Tree cookies

Seeds

Nuts

Grass

Flowers

Cattails

Milkweed pods

Roots

Stems

Walnuts

Nut husks

Potted plants

Greenery

Dried grains/flowers/spices

Plant samples

Pumpkins

Bird seed

Bark samples

Animals

Humans

Hands

Our bodies

The brain

Bones

Invertebrates

Feathers

Sand dollars

Earthworms

Soil

Dead animals

Animal parts: feathers, shed skins, bones, antlers, fur

Real bugs

Caterpillars

Insect specimens

Butterflies for observation

Fur samples

Leather samples

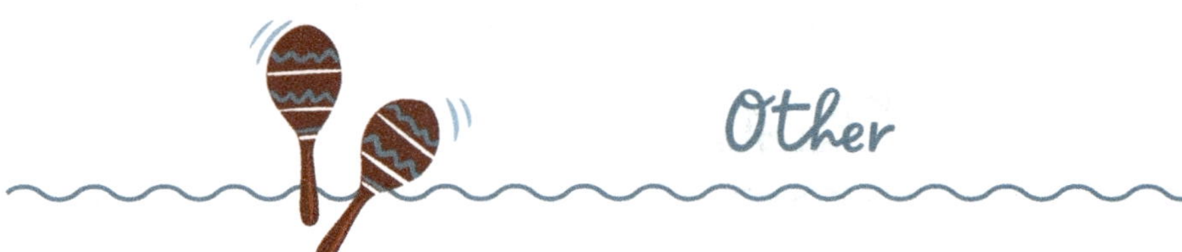

Other

Silks

Paints

Clay

Recyclables

Cardboard

Plastic bottles

Plastic caps

Plastic, wooden, or soapstone animal figurines

Silk flowers

Kinetic sand

Musical instruments

Nature

Ice

Snow

Snowflakes

Icicles

Water

Sand

Shells

Soil (of different textures)

Mud

Lichen

Fungi

Rocks

Gemstones

Sea glass

APPENDIX C

Professional Learning Communities: Like a Book Club for Enthusiasts

As you continue your journey of discovery through living loose parts, we strongly recommend you find or form a group of like-minded individuals to serve as supporters to encourage and inspire along the way. Each time you meet, virtually or in-person, plan two or three questions to guide your discussions. Good questions to spark meaningful conversations can be as simple as:

- What are you learning?
- Where have you gotten stuck?
- What inspired you today?
- What made you laugh?
- What made you think?
- What do you want to learn next?
- What have you been reading?
- What have you been writing?
- What have you noticed?
- What do you wonder?
- How do you plan to challenge yourself?
- How can you find out more?

References and Recommended Reading

Acadiana Center for the Arts and Lafayette Parish School System. 2020. "PACE Online: Shadow Dance: Light and its Relationship to Objects." Acadiana Center for the Arts. https://www.youtube.com/watch?v=yxDcfzAVGzI

Adams, Dylan, and Tonia Gray. 2023. "An Exploration of How the Disruption of Mainstream Schooling during the COVID-19 Crisis Provided Opportunities That We Can Learn from So That We May Improve Our Future Relationship with the More-Than-Human World." *SN Social Sciences* 3(1): 18. doi:10.1007/s43545-022-00588-1

Behr, Gregg, and Ryan Rydzewski. 2021. *When You Wonder, You're Learning: Mr. Rogers' Enduring Lessons for Raising Creative, Curious, Caring Kids.* New York: Hachette.

Brogan, Caroline. 2022. "Engineers Uncover Secret 'Thinking' Behind Dandelions' Seed Dispersal." Imperial. https://www.imperial.ac.uk/news/236934/engineers-uncover-secret-thinking-behind-dandelions/#:~:text=Known%20for%20their%20fluffiness%20and,birds%2C%20butterflies%2C%20and%20moths.&text=Their%20seeds%20are%20some%20of,as%20far%20as%20100%20kilometres

Carson, Rachel. 1956. *The Sense of Wonder: A Celebration of Nature for Parents and Children.* New York: HarperCollins Publishers.

Carson, Rachel. 1962. *Silent Spring.* Boston: Houghton Mifflin Company.

Centers for Disease Control and Prevention. 2023. "Fast Facts: Preventing Adverse Childhood Experiences." CDC.gov. https://www.cdc.gov/violenceprevention/aces/fastfact.html

Charney, Sara A., Stephen M. Camarata, and Alexander Chern. 2021. "Potential Impact of the COVID-19 Pandemic on Communication and Language Skills in Children." *Otolaryngology—Head and Neck Surgery* 165(1): 1–2.

Clark, Alison. 2023. *Slow Knowledge and the Unhurried Child: Time for Slow Pedagogies in Early Childhood Education.* New York: Routledge.

Coyle, Kevin J. 2017. *Digital Technology's Role in Connecting Children and Adults to Nature and the Outdoors.* National Wildlife Federation. https://www.nwf.org/~/media/PDFs/Kids-and-Nature/NWF_Role-of-Technology-in-Connecting-Kids-to-Nature_6-30_lsh.ashx

Dargatz, Peter. 2021. "Nature's Dozen." *Teaching Off Trail: My Classroom's Nature Transformation through Play*. St. Paul, MN: Redleaf Press.

Davidson, Bridget, et al. 2021. "Risk and Resilience of Well-Being in Caregivers of Young Children in Response to the COVID-19 Pandemic." *Translational Behavioral Medicine* 11(2): 305–313. https://doi.org/10.1093/tbm/ibaa124

Donnelly, Robin, and Harry Patrinos. 2022. "Learning Loss during COVID-19: An Early Systematic Review." *Prospects* 51(4): 601–609. doi:10.1007/s11125-021-09582-6

Doyle, Terry. 2011. *Learner-Centered Teaching: Putting the Research on Learning into Practice*. London, UK: Routledge.

Egan, Suzanne M., et al. 2021. "Missing Early Education and Care During the Pandemic: The Socio-Emotional Impact of the COVID-19 Crisis on Young Children." *Early Childhood Education Journal* 49(5): 925–934. doi:10.1007/s10643-021-01193-2

Fitzgerald, Meghan. 2023. "Supporting Sensory Development in Kids." Blog, *Tinkergarten*, August 16. https://tinkergarten.com/blog/8-easy-ways-to-support-sensory-development.

Forman, George, and David Kuschner. 1983. *The Child's Construction of Knowledge: Piaget for Teaching Children*. Washington, DC: NAEYC.

Fox, Heather, et al. 2022. *Environmental Kinship Guide*. Environmental Kinship International. https://environmentalkinship.org/

Fravel, Nicole. 2017. "Building Children's Observation Skills with Sit Spots." Oregon Association for the Education of Young Children. https://www.oraeyc.org/single-post/2017/12/11/Build-Childrens-Observation-Skills-with-Sit-Spots

Fthenakis, Lisa. 2018. "How Many Objects Does the Smithsonian Have?" Smithsonian Institution Archives. https://siarchives.si.edu/blog/how-many-objects-does-smithsonian-have

Galinsky, Ellen. 2010. *Mind in the Making: The Seven Essential Life Skills Every Child Needs*. New York: HarperStudio.

Gull, Carla. 2013. "Ex Quotient: Are You Willing to Fail?" Blog, *Inside Outside Michiana*, September 15. http://insideoutsidemichiana.blogspot.com/2013/09/ex-quotient-are-you-willing-to-fail.html

Gull, Carla. 2015. "On Meadowview Street: A Book Review." Blog, *Inside Outside Michiana*, April 16.

Gull, Carla. 2018. "Nature Art Inspiration." Blog, *Inside Outside Michiana*, January 31.

Gull, Carla. 2022a. "Deconstructive Play." Loose Parts Nature Play. https://loosepartsnatureplay.org/2022/07/24/deconstructive-play/

Gull, Carla. 2022b. "Loose Parts Nature Play Kits: Something for Everyone!" Podcast, *Loose Parts Nature Play*, June 24. https://loosepartsnatureplay.libsyn.com/loose-parts-nature-play-kits-something-for-everyone

Gull, Carla. 2023a. "Apps and Technology to Get Outside." Indiana Children and Nature Network. Webinar. https://youtu.be/JZ2W0bcb_H4?si=nBGBZ6fRec0ZdJi1

Gull, Carla. 2023b. "Embracing Fire as a Loose Part." Loose Parts Nature Play podcast. https://loosepartsnatureplay.libsyn.com/embracing-fire-as-a-loose-part

Gull, Carla, Jessica Bogunovich, Suzanne Levenson Goldstein, and Tricia Rosengarten. 2019. "Definitions of Loose Parts in Early Childhood Outdoor Classrooms: A Scoping Review." *International Journal of Early Childhood Environmental Education* 6(3): 37–52.

Gull, Carla, Suzanne Levenson Goldstein, and Tricia Rosengarten. 2018. "Benefits and Risks of Tree Climbing on Child Development and Resiliency." *International Journal of Early Childhood Environmental Education* 5(2): 10–29.

Gull, Carla, Suzanne Levenson Goldstein, and Tricia Rosengarten. 2020. "Early Childhood Educators' Perspectives on Tree Climbing." *International Journal of Early Childhood Environmental Education* 8(1): 26–43.

Gull, Carla, Suzanne Levenson Goldstein, and Tricia Rosengarten. 2023. "Celebrating Special Days with a Loose Parts Mindset." Exchange. https://hub.exchangepress.com/articles-on-demand/10715/

Hammond, Zaretta. 2014. *Culturally Responsive Teaching and the Brain: Promoting Authentic Engagement and Rigor among Culturally and Linguistically Diverse Students*. Thousand Oaks, CA: Corwin.

Hanfstingl, Barbara, Ana Arzenšek, Jan Apschner, and Katharina I. Gölly. 2021. "Assimilation and Accommodation: A Systematic Review of the Last Two Decades." *European Psychologist* 27(4): 320–337.

Haughey, Sally. n.d. "The Benefits of Clay Play: Understanding the Exploration Stage of Children." Wunderled. https://wunderled.com/blog/the-benefits-of-clay-play-understanding-the-exploration-stage-of-children/

Haupt, Angela. 2023. "Your Houseplants Have Some Powerful Health Benefits. *Time*, March 2. https://time.com/6258638/indoor-plants-health-benefits/

Hughes, Anita M. n.d. "Elinor Goldschmied and Treasure Baskets." Froebel Trust. https://www.froebel.org.uk/training-and-resources/elinor-goldschmied-treasure-baskets

Indiana Administrative Code. n.d. 410 IAC 33-4-7 Animals. https://www.in.gov/health/eph/files/A00330.pdf

Kashdan, Todd. 2018. "What Are the Five Dimensions of Curiosity? A Comprehensive New Model to Understand and Measure Curiosity." *Psychology Today*. https://psychologytoday.com/us/blog/curious/201801/what-are-the-five-dimensions-of-curiosity

Keeler, Rusty. 2020a. *Adventures in Risky Play: What Is Your Yes?* Lincoln, NE: Exchange Press.

Keeler, Rusty 2020b. "Risk-Benefit Analysis Tips." Exchange Every Day. https://www.exchangepress.com/eed/issue/5280

Kiewra, Christine, and Ellen Veselack. 2016. "Playing with Nature: Supporting Preschoolers' Creativity in Natural Outdoor Classrooms." *International Journal of Early Childhood Environmental Education* 4(1): 70–95.

Learning in Places. n.d. "Family Seasonal Storyline." Learning in Places. http://learninginplaces.org/family-seasonal-storyline/

Lee, Kate E., et al. 2015. "40-Second Green Roof Views Sustain Attention: The Role of Micro-Breaks in Attention Restoration." *Journal of Environmental Psychology* 42: 182–189.

Louv, Richard. 2019. *Our Wild Calling: How Connecting with Animals Can Transform Our Lives—and Save Theirs.* Chapel Hill, NC: Algonquin Books.

Mason, Lisa, et al. 2022. "Short-Term Exposure to Nature and Benefits for Students' Cognitive Performance: A Review." *Educational Psychology Review* 34: 609–647.

Measimer, Ken, dir. 2015. 2015 *Timpani Toy Study: Toys That Inspire Mindful Play and Nurture Imagination.* Film. Eastern Connecticut State University. https://www.easternct.edu/center-for-early-childhood-education/timpani/timpani-2015.html

Melson, Gail. 2013. "Nature Nurture: Children Can Become Stewards of Our Fragile Planet." Blog, *Psychology Today*, April 11. https://www.psychologytoday.com/us/blog/why-the-wild-things-are/201304/nature-nurture

Merriam-Webster. "Praxis." Merriam-Webster.com Dictionary. https://www.merriam-webster.com/dictionary/praxis

Merry Lea. n.d. Sit Spot Pedagogy. https://www.goshen.edu/merrylea/wp-content/uploads/2022/07/Sit-spot_final.pdf

Monsalvatge, Laura, Kris Long, and Lilia DiBello. 2013. "Turning Our World of Learning Inside Out!" *Dimensions of Early Childhood* 41(3): 23–30.

Montessori, Maria. 2012. *The 1946 London Lectures*. The Montessori Series. Vol. 17. Edited by Annette Haines. Laren, Netherlands: Montessori-Pierson Publishing Company.

National Association of Biology Teachers. 2019. *The Use of Animals in the Biology Education*. Position statement. https://nabt.org/Position-Statements-The-Use-of-Animals-in-Biology-Education

NGSS Lead States. 2013. *Next Generation Science Standards: For States, By States*. Washington, DC: The National Academies Press. https://doi.org/10.17226/18290

Nicholson, Simon. 1970. "The Planning and Design of the Recreation Environment." *What Do Playgrounds Teach?* Davis, CA: University Extension, University of California, Davis.

Nicholson, Simon. 1971. "How Not to Cheat Children: The Theory of Loose Parts." *Landscape Architecture* 62(1): 30–34.

North American Reggio Alliance. 2012. *Shadow Stories.* DVD. North American Reggio Alliance. https://www.store.reggioalliance.org/products/shadow-stories-poetics-of-an-encounter-between-science-and-narration

Paley, Vivian G. 1987. *Wally's Stories: Conversations in the Kindergarten.* Cambridge, MA: Harvard University Press.

Paley, Vivan G. 1991. *The Boy Who Would Be a Helicopter: The Uses of Storytelling in the Classroom.* Rev. ed. Cambridge, MA: Harvard University Press.

Papert, Seymour. 1999. "Child Psychologist Jean Piaget." *Time.* https://content.time.com/time/subscriber/article/0,33009,990617,00.html

Penn State Extension. 2023. "Play with Clay." Penn State Extension. https://extension.psu.edu/programs/betterkidcare/early-care/tip-pages/all/play-with-clay

Penrose, William O. 1980. "Piaget and the Teaching of Mathematics." Childhood Education 57(1): 22–25.

Pollinator Partnership. 2024. "Pollinators Need You. You Need Pollinators." Pollinator Partnership. https://www.pollinator.org/pollinators

Robertson, Juliet. 2017. *Messy Maths: A Playful, Outdoor Approach for Early Years.* Carmarthen, Wales, UK: Independent Thinking Press.

Rodenburg, Jacob. 2022. *The Book of Nature Connection: 70 Sensory Activities for All Ages.* Gabriola Island, BC: New Society Publishers.

Rukeyser, Muriel. 1968. *The Speed of Darkness.* New York: Random House.

Sanchez, Anita. n.d. "Hello, Puddle! Educator's Guide." Anita Sanchez. https://anitasanchez.com/hello-puddle/hello-puddle-educators-guide/

Sandseter, Ellen B. H. 2007. "Categorising Risky Play—How Can We Identify Risk-Taking in Children's Play?" *European Early Childhood Education Research Journal* 15(2): 237–252.

Sappenfield, Julia. n.d. The Importance of Stick Play. Boston Outdoor Preschool Network. https://www.bopn.org/blog/the-importance-of-stick-play

Selly, Patty Born. 2014. *Connecting Animals and Children in Early Childhood.* St. Paul, MN: Redleaf Press.

Sifferlin, Alexandra. 2016. "The Healing Power of Nature." *Time*, July 14. https://time.com/4405827/the-healing-power-of-nature/

Skar, Gustaf B. U., Steve Graham, and Alan Huebner. 2022. "Learning Loss during the COVID-19 Pandemic and the Impact of Emergency Remote Instruction on First Grade Students' Writing: A Natural Experiment. *Journal of Educational Psychology* 114(7): 1553–1566.

Sobel, David. 1996. *Beyond Ecophobia: Reclaiming the Heart in Nature Education*. Great Barrington, MA: Orion Society.

Spencer, John. 2018. "How Nature Inspires Better Design (and What This Means for Students)." Medium. https://medium.com/@spencerideas/how-nature-inspires-better-design-and-what-this-means-for-students-7a72cb74cce4

Tinkergarten. (2024). "Parts and Wholes." Highlights. https://tinkergarten.com/activities/parts-and-wholes

Veselack, Ellen, Lisa Cain-Chang, and Dana L. Miller. 2009. "Young Children Develop Foundational Skills Through Child-initiated Experiences in a Nature Explore Classroom: A Single Case Study in La Cañada, California." Dimensions Educational Research Foundation. https://dimensionsfoundation.org/wp-content/uploads/2016/07/skillslacanadaca_10.pdf

Warden, Claire. 2022. *Green Teaching: Nature Pedagogies for Climate Change and Sustainability*. London, UK: Corwin.

Wilhelm, Laura. 2017. *Treasure Basket Explorations: Heuristic Learning for Infants and Toddlers*. Lewisville, NC: Gryphon House.

World Economic Forum. 2019. "Fewer Children Than Ever Know the Names for Plants and Animals." World Economic Forum. https://www.weforum.org/agenda/2019/09/children-are-forgetting-the-names-for-plants-and-animals/

Index

D

E

F

G

H

I

L

M

N

O

P